EUROPE

THE PLACES WE LOVE

Apple picking at Hotel Skeppsholmen, in Stockholm, Sweden.

EUROPE
THE PLACES WE LOVE

ISBN 978-1-932624-39-7
Published by American Express
Publishing Corporation
1120 Avenue of the Americas
New York, New York 10036

Distributed by Charlesbridge Publishing
85 Main Street, Watertown, Massachusetts 02472

Printed in Canada

The dining room at Maison Trévier,
in France's Rhône Valley.

Sakiz Ana, a
restaurant in
Bodrum, Turkey.

contents

KEY TO THE HOTEL PRICE ICONS $ UNDER $250 $$ $250–$499 $$$ $500–$749 $$$$ $750–$999 $$$$$ $1,000 AND UP
KEY TO THE DINING PRICE ICONS ✗ UNDER $25   ✗✗ $25–$74   ✗✗✗ $75–$149   ✗✗✗✗ $150–$299   ✗✗✗✗✗ $300 AND UP

The pool area and gardens at Villa Gallici, in Aix-en-Provence, France.

introduction

SOME THINGS REMAIN CONSTANT, DESPITE THE fast-changing map of the world, as hot spots come and go and geopolitical events remake destinations and borders. Take Europe, for example, which is cozily familiar to many American travelers, whose roots may extend deep into the Continent, and who may have explored its attractions many times before. Yet for art and architecture; cultural opportunities, from museums to dance and music; and history, Europe continues to hold endless allure.

With that in mind—and to celebrate *Travel + Leisure*'s 40th anniversary—we've created *Europe: The Places We Love*, a comprehensive guide to the enduringly exciting and newly thrilling locations that inspire us from across the Atlantic, with the practical details you need to plan your own trips abroad. The journey begins in that most iconic of European cities—and a favorite of ours—with a New York City transplant's revelation of her favorite haunts in "Insider's Paris" (page 12). It's an instance where the intimate and the everyday—the city's private face rather than the one put on for visitors—shine. We also have adventures of a different sort, with Barneys creative ambassador-at-large Simon Doonan's gambol on the island of Capri, off Italy's Amalfi Coast (page 72), to seek out the ultimate in seaside luxury.

When it comes to real-time immediacy and authenticity—a detail on which *Travel + Leisure* readers are placing more and more emphasis—you'll find plenty of it here. *Europe: The Places We Love* offers up stories such as "Barcelona by Design" (page 22), with the kind of fresh and knowing information that could only come from locals, and "Tips from the Tastemakers" (page 170), where three creative professionals describe the shops, restaurants, galleries, and performance spaces that make their home cities special. For those in search of still-emerging destinations, we explore the Baltic Coast in Latvia and Estonia (page 80), uncover some of the Continent's least traveled roads in our spotlight on secret villages (page 50), and investigate the unexpected yet much-heralded culinary scene in Iceland (page 130).

There are also fresh takes on classic itineraries and destinations, from an update on one of England's most quintessential gardens to a week spent sampling the epic flavors that abound in Tuscany. Witness "Rome's Green Empire" (page 64), a surprisingly peaceful look beyond the Eternal City's well-worn landmarks to its transformative green spaces, and "St. Petersburg Modern" (page 182), a 21st-century view of Russia's new culture capital.

But for all the decidedly modern people and places you find there, visiting Europe inevitably involves interacting with history. As you'll see throughout this book, even when dining at a cutting-edge restaurant or shopping in the boutique of the moment, you may well be overlooking an ancient cobblestoned street, a little-known piazza, or a grand boulevard that has always been there—solid and reassuring. My own vacation plans regularly include Europe, despite the world's many other seductive options. Try as I might, I just can't stay away.

NANCY NOVOGROD EDITOR-IN-CHIEF

Chef Sébastien Guénard
at his bistro Miroir, in Paris's
Abbesses district.

city streets

Posing on a bench at Paris's Parc Monceau, in the Ternes district. Opposite: A view of the city's mansard roofs.

INSIDER'S PARIS

BY ALEXANDRA MARSHALL
PHOTOGRAPHED BY RICHARD TRUSCOTT

I WAS ONLY SUPPOSED TO STAY FOR TWO MONTHS. IT WAS EARLY 2006, my father had just passed away, and I was courting massive burnout. When a saintly friend offered me a free room in his three-bedroom apartment in St.-Germain-des-Prés, I booked my ticket. Okay, I thought. Get away, learn a little French, smell the rosé, and come back fresh. But Paris had other plans for me. The way the apricot light at sunset bounced off its pale façades; the slower pace of life; the disdain for hysterical consumerism and the workaholism it requires; the tragic, fascinating history and the civic pride that comes with having survived it; the neighborhood markets, the organic markets, even the supermarkets, filled with readily available *terroir*: before my sojourn was up, I was hooked.

As grateful as I was for the free digs, St.-Germain is a better neighborhood for finding a luxury handbag than a couple of lemons and a six-pack of Kronenbourg. But the perch I settled on, in Montmartre's little village of Abbesses, is fit for my kind of living: relaxed, friendly, and pleasantly cacophonous. With every passing day, my roots grow deeper. Despite the bureaucracy (which is even worse than people say), the occasional explosions of nastiness (Parisian manners are either baroque or shockingly bad), and the weird in-between-ness of expat life, it would take a government intervention to get me to leave.

Opposite: À la Mère de Famille, a traditional confiserie in the Ninth Arrondissement.

In the time from being a visitor to setting up house, I've learned that the Paris I live in is a much lovelier place than the one I had ever known before. The city's deeply grooved tourist tracks—St.-Germain, the First, the Latin Quarter, the Champs-Élysées—have much worth seeing, but compared with the life I live in the 18th Arrondissement, they feel slick and prefab, like a gift set of experiences shoved brusquely through a revolving door. In spite of being the world's most visited urban center, and the proliferation of Subway sandwich shops, the occasional Starbucks, and all those homegrown luxury companies gone multinational, the city is fueled by mom-and-pop businesses that allow it to maintain a profoundly, sometimes anarchically, idiosyncratic character. During an interview I did with the British actress Jane Birkin recently, she joked that France is a nation of soloists, incapable of forming an orchestra, and this is especially true in the capital city, which houses 10 million of the country's boisterously unique, queue-jumping *citoyens*. The expressiveness, eccentricity, and drama on display here are rivaled only by New York City at its most vibrant. It's in the farther-flung corners, the parts of the city less manicured for the consumption of outsiders, where you find the earthiness that mellows that bad temper, and where you more clearly see what makes Paris one of the most authentically charming places on earth.

TIME FOR AN AMERICAN BAKERY METAPHOR: IMAGINE THE CINNAMON BUN–SHAPED MAP OF Paris. Now slice a large wedge from the top section. You'll end up cutting the Ninth, 10th, 17th, 18th, and 19th Arrondissements, or what Sébastien Guénard, the chef at the fêted Abbesses bistro Miroir, calls "*le grand quartier.*" In the short time since I've moved to the area, I've watched the steady onslaught of gentrification. The same is true for Pigalle and Notre-Dame-de-Lorette, just to the south; Batignolles, to the west (the rest of the 17th was already pretty haute-bourgeois); the Canal

St.-Martin, in the 10th; Belleville, in the 19th and 20th; and other areas in the 19th that surround the Parc des Buttes-Chaumont. I'll add the Oberkampf piece of the 11th to the east, too; though it's not geographically in *le grand quartier*, it shares the same earthy spirit.

As with so many "outer" neighborhoods that are now "in," the traditional working-class immigrant population of the northeast has been diluted by bohemian professionals and the small boutiques, organic food stores, and casual, food-fetishist bistros that nourish them. Turns out my new home shares a lot more than I realized with the Brooklyn I left. Yannick Flageul, an accessories designer and the creator of the indie perfume brand NSEW, could have his pick of neighborhoods in town but couldn't imagine living outside of Paris's most thriving immigrant hub, Belleville. The area is a tossed salad of Chinatown, souk, and ghetto, and its residents are fiercely loyal. "I love the intelligent human patchwork here," says Flageul, who has been living there for more than a decade. "We're artists and we're workers. We're trendy, sexy, ugly, gay, straight, Arab, Jewish, black, white, yellow. Life here is awesomely unstuffy."

That goes for the food, too. If you think back to the traditional stereotype of French restaurant dining, you'll envision grumpy, bow-tied waiters and a confusing array of silverware. All of this fusty silliness is now more and more easily avoided thanks to the "bistronomy" revolution so thoroughly chronicled by both the French and American press. Allow me to join in the adulation and note that *le grand quartier* and the 11th are home to some of the best examples of the phenomenon. Bistronomy is a back-to-basics movement that started with Yves Camdeborde's La Régalade in 1992 and continued in outlying neighborhoods where the chefs and owners themselves live. Generally, a restaurant in this genre serves under-$50 prix fixe menus prepared by young chefs who favor the finest small-producer ingredients and cut their teeth in haute establishments. Diners are either neighbors or those who play follow-the-chef along with the slavering food press and blogs such as lefooding.com. I fell in love with Miroir the first time I walked in the door and was greeted by the broad smile and neon-green Adidas of the owner's young wife, a former employee of the magnificent wine emporium Lavinia, who steered me through the small, refined *carte* as if I were an old friend. Then I ate their caramelized pork belly from the Basque producer Louis Ospital,

served au jus with roasted root vegetables. Cartoon hearts floated above my head, and soon the restaurant and I had each other on speed dial.

The upside of bistronomy is massive for the individualistic French: young restaurateurs need only toil at grand, Michelin-starred places long enough to learn something about polish and technique before jumping ship to a homier, more autonomous vessel. "I need to see the plates and talk to the guests," says Frédéric Hubig-Schall, the owner of the 11th Arrondissement's Astier, who previously worked with Yannick Alléno at Le Meurice. When Hubig-Schall and his partners took over the place in 2006, it was a corny café with a predictable meat-sauce-starch menu. They kept the down-at-the-heels décor, but upgraded the menu to include far finer examples of traditional French cooking. Astier's pressed beef cheek with a deviled egg is a prettier endeavor than the description might suggest, and its copious cheese plate and more than 350 choices of wine are worth lingering over much longer than the average lunchtime would allow. (Do clear your schedule; Hubig-Schall and his sommelier are usually in house at lunch, speak English, and love to chat.)

"When a restaurant is too big, there are too many people between you and the guest. A smaller scale means more pleasure and sensitivity," Hubig-Schall says. For Miroir's Guénard, grad school was Alain Ducasse's Aux Lyonnais and the Hôtel du Palais. One of Le Bistral's chefs trained at the Ritz. And at Le Bouchon et l'Assiette, in the 17th, it was Michel Sarran, Hôtel Le Bristol, and the Hôtel du Palais again. Here, the food is hearty and painstakingly sourced, with soft flashes of globalism—scallops in wispy ginger bouillon, velouté of garbanzo beans with *sobrasada* sausage, or rich *gâteau basque*. Even as more of these restaurants open, the shock of eating well for such little fuss and money somehow never wears off. And there's more: so in love with the high quality of their products are these restaurateurs that many of them have opened groceries (Le Bistral; Astier) and wine stores (Miroir) across the street or next door.

Indeed, a close cousin to bistronomy is a wave of wine bars with a similar approach to impeccable ingredients and low-key refinement. The Parisian wine bar—a working-class hangout with copious by-the-glass choices that thrives at lunchtime—seems like it's been with us forever. In fact, it's a creation of the post–World War II period, when France wrested its wine industry

back from the industrial swill it was producing during the war. In 1954, some Beaujolais producers started the Coupe du Meilleur Pot award, which is managed by the Académie Rabelais, a food society peopled by French critics and scholars. Its criteria nail the ideal wine bar equation: great wines by the glass, a favorable ratio of quality to price, and an in-house proprietor. That last element is crucial, as a jocular owner full of opinions is just as important as what's on tap.

You couldn't ask for better than Gilles Bénard at Quedubon, in the 19th, which opened in 2007. Minutes off the east side of the Buttes-Chaumont, with modern but warm interiors, Quedubon's list has some 150 *vins natures*, or beyond-organic wines untainted by additives or chemicals. If Bénard, a voluble leftist of the old school, is on site, and your French is passable, you're in for a good time. "People in Paris now are searching for quality and authenticity," he says. "Maybe it would have been easier for me to have opened in Sentier [the garment district in the Second Arrondissement], but the crowd that comes here is not coming by chance. Here we have a whole conversation with guests. We're doing real *sommellerie*, trying to transmit a culture." Bénard sings the praises of Olivier Camus' equally impressive Chapeau Melon, in Belleville, with about 200 natural wines and a similarly market-driven menu four nights a week. Honorable

mention also goes to fellow natural-wine vanguardists Le Verre Volé, near the Canal St.-Martin, and La Muse Vin, in the 11th.

For all of bistronomy's pleasures, nothing beats a picnic in one of the city's green spaces. The 61-acre Parc des Buttes-Chaumont is bohemian Paris's favorite spot. On the weekends, thanks to the wine-and-snack bar Rosa Bonheur, it's a major scene. If you're searching for an only-in-Paris experience, head to the Pavillon du Chemin de Fer, inside the park's southern border, well before dark, and make sure to get on the right side of the barricades the house erects around 7 p.m., when the party begins. Once the stanchions go up, those unlucky enough to be on the other side must wait in a brutally long line to get onto the patio (or catapult themselves over the barricades, as several girls in American Apparel rompers did the last time I was there). Under colored Christmas lights, a hip crowd—a mix of fashion, advertising, and art types—drinks enough rosé and eats enough saucisson to give a nutritionist fits.

Occupying a different spot on the socioeconomic spectrum is the majestic Parc Monceau, which lies between the 17th and the top of the Eighth in the fancy Ternes district. Every time I pass by the park's grand, gold-tipped, 19th-century gates, I am struck by the desire to walk barefoot. Planted in the English style,

Above, from left: Caramelized pork belly with roasted vegetables at Miroir; strolling near Rue de Bretagne, in the Marais.

AMB

18e Arr!

**RUE
NORVINS**

DESSERTS

Assiette de fromages	7,00	Gâteau aux pommes	6,80
Crème brûlée	6,30	Fromage blanc au miel	5,30
Mousse au chocolat	6,30		

GLACES

| Vanille, chocolat, fraise, café | 5,80 |
| Nougat glacé, coulis de framboise | 6,30 |

COUPES

| Café ou Chocolat Liégeois | 7,60 |

CRÊPES

Au Sucre	3,30	Au Nutella	6,00
À la confiture de fraise	6,00	Flambée au rhum	7,60
À la confiture d'abricot	6,00	Supplément Chantilly	1,00

CONSOM

DE C

BIE

BRUNE &

TELEP

the abundant flowers and trees feel a bit wilder than in your typically manicured French garden. International follies, such as a windmill and a Chinese fort, make for multiple jewel-box vistas. Nearby, on the Boulevard de Courcelles, are all the cheese, wine, and roast chicken you need for a stellar *déjeuner sur l'herbe*. There are few places where I'd rather spend hours lolling around among dogs and families.

For a slightly more structured experience, the Jardin des Plantes, on the border of the 13th and the Fifth, is pure magic. Created in 1635, the park includes a zoo, a natural history museum, and a sprawling botanical garden. I have spent hours in its Gallery of Paleontology and Comparative Anatomy sneaking camera-phone pictures of mutant animal skeletons and snapping the snow leopards and macaws in its sweet little zoo. Next to the park's western entrance on Rue Geoffroy St.-Hilaire is La Mosquée. The complex, one of the country's Muslim institutes, is actually the largest mosque in France and has a nice restaurant that opens onto a wide patio. A kaleidoscope of traditional Algerian tile, with exposed entrances that allow birds to fly through its halls, the restaurant serves so-so couscous and great mint tea and pastries.

I AM PROUD TO SAY I HAVE ALMOST SHED MY *new-yorquaise* shopping addiction. Almost. After all, Paris is, despite the natives' disinterest, a paradise for the acquisitive. Rather than endure the throngs at the *grands magasins* or on the Rue St.-Honoré, my first stop is always the Galeries du Palais-Royal. It's got excellent shops along the garden behind the palace itself: Stella McCartney, Marc Jacobs, the glove maker Mary Beyer, Rick Owens, vintage couturier Didier Ludot, and the accessories genius Pierre Hardy, who also designs for Balenciaga and Hermès. In spite of its dead-central location, the Palais-Royal is quiet and calm. This is partly due to its status as a historically protected monument (it was built as the home of Cardinal Richelieu in the early 1600's): the companies it houses can never eclipse the structure itself. In most cases, the original shop signage remains virtually unchanged from a century ago, so it's the windows, far recessed under those gorgeous colonnades, that have to do the talking, and most of them choose to whisper. You could visit the gardens and almost not know you were in the city's coolest de facto luxury mall.

Boutiques in neighborhoods that don't scream "Shopping!" help to thwart the conveyor-belt feeling, too. Spree, in Abbesses, offers a mix of European and Asian labels (Isabel Marant; Martin Margiela 6; Helmut Lang; Tsumori Chisato; Carven) casually strewn over Midcentury furniture, and it still feels fresh to my seen-it-all American friends. The shop's friendly owners, Bruno Hadjadj and Roberta Oprandi, used to live across the street, but they've transformed their former house into an art and furniture gallery called Papiers Peints. It's named after the sign on the building's façade, which was designed by Le Corbusier for what was once a wallpaper store.

Then again, there are times you just need to go to the Marais. The historically orthodox-Jewish neighborhood is one of a growing number in Paris that allows shops to stay open on Sunday, and on the weekends, the place is as densely packed as the Champs-Élysées. In the past decade the throngs have been coming for hipster Gallic sportswear (Comptoir des Cotonniers; Maje; Zadig & Voltaire), but I am a bigger fan of the area's vintage shopping. I'm not talking so much about precious, forbiddingly expensive bijou stores but the down-and-dirtier *friperies*, or thrift stores, such as Free'P'Star. A recent houseguest of mine runs a vintage business out of Nashville, and she shopped the boutique's airy 1980's-era print dresses so hard that she'll be fully stocked until next season.

In high-density situations like this, fast sustenance is key. Years ago, the French husband of one of my oldest friends laid down his *boulangerie* rule: if it is great at breads and savories, it will not be so at pastries, and vice versa. He lives in the Marais, near Pain de Sucre, and since it opened in 2004, the place has changed his mind. Didier Mathray and Nathalie Robert's salty, flaky, olive-oil brioche is what first turned my head; their *pirouette pomme*, with crunchy almond crust, pistachio-and-lime cream, and apples caramelized with rosemary, made me a believer. If you're brave enough to attack the *grands magasins*, know that the food halls at the Galeries Lafayette and Printemps are both extraordinary, though not exactly Zen. But À la Mère de Famille, a few blocks east of the department stores, is everything you want a traditional confiserie to be: full of froufrou offerings and temptations at every turn. Traditional Breton *caramels au fleur de sel* often lack the chewy texture they master here,

Opposite, clockwise from top left: A mannequin at the Abbesses boutique Spree; Neoclassical apartments in the Marais; the neighborhood's café culture; a restaurant on Rue Norvins, in the 18th.

and their dense, flavorful chocolate-almond ice cream is a killer.

Paris has been on a hospitality roll lately; take advantage and book a hotel in the Ninth. In the shadow of the Arc de Triomphe, there's the Intercontinental Paris Avenue Marceau, with its careful and chic assemblage of design furniture and modern art. Right off the Champs-Élysées is Grace Leo's cheerfully sleek Hôtel Beauchamp, and there's something of an Asian invasion afoot with the arrival of Raffles's Royal Monceau, Shangri-La, and Mandarin Oriental; in 2013, the Peninsula will open.

Grand hotels have their charms, but staying at one of the *quartier*'s crop of boutique lodgings means the best of both worlds can be yours. You're in *le grand quartier*, but convenient to the central city's monuments. When Hôtel Amour made its debut in 2006, its rock-bottom prices, cheeky décor, hourly-rate policy, and boldface-name patrons shook up the district. Now, just a few blocks away, is the Hôtel Joyce. It doesn't have the fashionable pedigree of Amour, whose owners are the nightlife

kings Mr. André and Thierry Costes. Nor does it have the youthful crowds. But it's a poppy, quirky newcomer that has immaculate, affordable rooms with great beds and lots of light. A few minutes southeast is the boutique Hôtel Jules, also a Grace Leo–managed property, with small but well-kitted rooms and a lobby that feels like a space-age library. Finally, almost across the street from the migraine-inducing department stores on the Boulevard Haussmann is the neo-Baroque opulence of the Banke Hôtel, with all the jewel tones and gilt accents of the First Arrondissement's Hôtel Costes sans the appalling service. For the most part, Parisian hotels have their manners together much more than the shops and restaurants. But don't expect the city as a whole to bend too much to fit foreign expectations. If it weren't intransigent, it wouldn't be Paris. Yes, you occasionally have to endure a terse sigh or peevish cab driver. But in a town with sculpture in every doorway, 10 kinds of organic smoked salmon in every supermarket, and a value system that prizes sensual pleasure above all, you will always come out ahead. ✚

resources

STAY

Banke Hôtel 20 Rue La Fayette, Ninth Arr.; 33-1/55-33-22-22; derbyhotels.com; doubles from $$.

Hôtel Amour 8 Rue Navarin, Ninth Arr.; 33-1/48-78-31-80; hotelamourparis.fr; doubles from $.

Hôtel Joyce 29 Rue La Bruyère, Ninth Arr.; 33-1/55-07-00-01; astotel.com; doubles from $$.

Hôtel Jules 49-51 Rue La Fayette, Ninth Arr.; 33-1/42-85-05-44; hoteljules.com; doubles from $.

EAT

À la Mère de Famille
33-35 Rue du Faubourg, Ninth Arr.; 33-1/47-70-83-69; pastries for two ✘.

Astier 44 Rue Jean-Pierre Timbaud, 11th Arr.; 33-1/43-57-16-35; lunch for two ✘✘✘.

Chapeau Melon
92 Rue Rébeval, 19th Arr.; 33-1/42-02-68-60; dinner for two ✘✘✘.

La Mosquée 39 Rue Geoffroy St.-Hilaire, Fifth Arr.; 33-1/43-31-18-14; tea for two ✘.

La Muse Vin 101 Rue de Charonne, 11th Arr.; 33-1/40-09-93-05; lunch for two ✘✘.

La Régalade 49 Ave. Jean Moulin, 14th Arr.; 33-1/45-45-68-58; dinner for two ✘✘✘.

Le Bistral 80 Rue Lemercier, 17th Arr.; 33-1/42-63-59-61; dinner for two ✘✘✘.

Le Bouchon et l'Assiette
127 Rue Cardinet, 17th Arr.; 33-1/42-27-83-93; dinner for two ✘✘✘.

Le Verre Volé 67 Rue de Lancry, 10th Arr.; 33-1/48-03-17-34; lunch for two ✘✘.

Miroir 94 Rue des Martyrs, 18th Arr.; 33-1/46-06-50-73; dinner for two ✘✘✘.

Pain de Sucre
14 Rue Rambuteau, Third Arr.; 33-1/45-74-68-92; pastries for two ✘.

Quedubon 22 Rue du Plateau, 19th Arr.; 33-1/42-38-18-65; dinner for two ✘✘✘.

Rosa Bonheur 2 Allée de la Cascade, 19th Arr; 33-1/42-00-00-45; wine and snacks for two ✘✘.

SHOP

Free'P'Star 8 Rue Ste.-Croix de la Bretonnerie, Fourth Arr.; 33-1/42-76-03-72

Galeries du Palais-Royal
6 Rue de Montpensier, First Arr.; 33-1/47-03-92-16.

Papiers Peints 11 Rue de la Vieuville, 18th Arr.; 33-1/42-59-99-90.

Spree 16 Rue de la Vieuville, 18th Arr.; 33-1/42-23-41-40.

BARCELONA
BY DESIGN

With its tradition of experimentation, Barcelona has long been at the forefront
of Mediterranean culture. Today, that storied legacy continues. At one end
of tony Passeig de Gràcia, the Carrer Séneca area offers an eclectic mix of colorful
boutiques, chic ateliers, and creative restaurants for in-the-know urbanites.

This page, clockwise from above: Children's clothing at Nobodinoz; a dress by Lydia Delgado; Roig Robí's Spanish wine collection; Nobodinoz's "Amsterdam" cabinet collection by Kast van een Huis.

Carrer de Gràcia

Carrer Gran de Gràcia

Carrer de la Riera de Sant Miquel

Passeig de Gràcia

Carrer Séneca

Via Augusta

Avinguda Diagonal

0 ————— 200 ft (61 m)

Cucharada

Flowy 1970's vintage caftans and cocktail dresses share the racks with Cucharada's own line of handmade leather bags and accessories. 15 Carrer de la Riera de Sant Miquel; 34/93-237-8093; cucharadabcn.blogspot.com.

Galería Miquel Alzueta

Set in a former basement textile shop, the loftlike gallery showcases cutting-edge international and Spanish artists such as local painter Miguel Macaya. 9-11 Carrer Séneca; 34/93-238-9750; galeria miquelalzueta.com.

Lydia Delgado

This crimson-walled shop stocks Delgado's signature black and ivory separates and colorful knits. 21 Carrer de Minerva; 34/93-415-9998; lydiadelgado.es.

Nobodinoz

A well-curated collection of products for tots—playful floral-print suitcases; custom furniture—is hand-picked by French émigré Murielle Bressan. 9 Carrer Séneca; 34/93-368-6335; nobodinoz.com.

Ox Mobiliari

Two spacious floors house Midcentury Modern furniture

and lighting, plus glass objets d'art. Look for curvaceous wooden chairs by Danish designer Hans Wegner. 8 Carrer Séneca; 34/65-069-1290.

Palau Antiguitats

Known for his discerning eye, art and antiques dealer Albert Martí Palau runs a gallery that has rare prints by Spain's modern and old masters, including pieces by Goya. 1 Carrer de Gràcia; 34/93-237-6158; palauantiguitats.com.

Roig Robí

Barcelona's sophisticated set comes for the classic Catalan fare, such as fluffy *buñuelos de bacalao* (cod fritters) and Iberian suckling pig, served on a garden terrace. 20 Carrer Séneca; 34/93-218-9222; lunch for two **XXX**.

This page, clockwise from top left: Lydia Delgado's studio; a brass Louis Weisdorf lamp at Ox Mobiliari; the store's home furnishings; vintage dresses at Cucharada; Cucharada's patchwork leather bag; an oil painting by Francesc Labarta at Palau Antiguitats; Galería Miquel Alzueta's showroom.

LONDON'S NEXT GREAT NEIGHBORHOOD

BY MARK ELLWOOD
PHOTOGRAPHED BY REBECCA LEWIS

J UST NORTH OF SOHO, NEAR BUSTLING OXFORD STREET, SITS central London's hidden neighborhood: Fitzrovia. Home to louche, boho types in the late 19th century (the Pre-Raphaelites and Oscar Wilde lounged in its bars), Fitzrovia's leafy streets are lined with Edwardian-era apartments, Neoclassical mansions, and onetime warehouses. It hasn't always been so appealing: 30 years ago when my father, an artist, bought a printing works in a mews to convert into a studio, Fitzrovia had become a grubby, rundown area. Vendors sold cars from the streets, fashion companies used warehouses for wholesale showrooms, and the only landmark was the *Transformers*-like British Telecom Tower, looming over it all. But in recent years, it has undergone an astonishing, if discreet, revival. Tired of the over-gentrified East End, gallery owners have been eyeing Fitzrovia for its cheap rents and soaring spaces, and the arrival of top-flight destinations has helped spark the neighborhood's renaissance.

An example of Fitzrovia's new artistic lifeblood, Alison Jacques worked as a curator for the British School at Rome before opening her first London space in a Mayfair town house in 2004, but three years later decamped to a roomier 3,600-square-foot space here. Jacques's stable of artists blends the media-savvy and controversial (Ryan McGinley and Robert Mapplethorpe, whose estate she has managed since 1999) with pop culture favorites like Brazilian artist Lygia Clark (famous for her interactive exhibits) and collage maestro Paul Morrison. Another London gallerist, socialite Pilar Corrias, launched her namesake 3,800-square-foot venue to coincide with the Frieze Art Fair in 2008. Her roster includes Scottish conceptual artist Charles Avery and Berlin-based Keren Cytter, who is known for her narrative film and video works. Through Miuccia Prada, a client, Corrias tapped Rem Koolhaas to reimagine a leather showroom as a gallery with 16-foot ceilings and movable walls that accommodate monolithic art. On nearby Rathbone Place, the five-floor Lazarides occupies a Georgian town house that was once a brothel. The notorious, headline-grabbing gallery is run by Steve Lazarides, the onetime art director of London's now-defunct *SleazeNation* magazine. He was the first person to print a poster by

Opposite: The Yorkshire Grey
pub, on Langham Street.

media-shy graffiti artist Banksy and helped make him a global phenomenon. (Brangelina and Christina Aguilera have bought Banksy works from him.) Lazarides is also known for prankish, punk artists with a wicked wit, such as Jonathan Yeo, who makes detailed collage portraits of politicians using cutouts from vintage porn magazines. East End mainstay Stuart Shave/Modern Art deserted the Vyner Street neighborhood to open a 6,500-square-foot gallery in Fitzrovia designed by architect David Kohn. You'll find works here by talents such as sculptor David Altmejd, Canada's erstwhile Venice Biennale entry, and figurative painter Nigel Cooke.

With the art scene thriving, new restaurants, bars, and hotels have followed. From wallet-friendly lunches to late-night tapas, Fitzrovia's dining spots run the gamut. The exceedingly affordable Tex-Mex restaurant, Benito's Hat, is a favorite lunch place for gallerinas on the go thanks to the oversize burritos, made to order with chile-and-achiote braised chicken or grilled zucchini, chayote squash, and peppers; all the chiles and tomatillos used are sourced directly from a local farm. Lantana, a lovingly run café tucked away on a quiet pedestrian side street, showcases the work of emerging photographers like Anne-Caroline Morice and artists such as Kate Macleod. Check out the menu scrawled on the chalkboard in front—a recent one included the BERT (bacon, egg, rocket, and tomato) sandwich and corn fritters with sliced avocado. A buzzing tapas joint down the street, the bi-level Salt Yard is rustic and romantic, decorated with deep red walls and wooden tables. The kitchen dishes up homey plates such as confit of pork belly atop rosemary-infused cannellini beans, or zucchini flowers stuffed with Monte Enebro cheese, deep fried and drizzled with honey. The well-priced wine list offers select reds and whites from Italy and Spain. But if a picnic in nearby Regent's Park is more your speed, pick up a hamper filled with coffee and croissants at the deli in the sprawling Villandry, London's answer to Dean & DeLuca. The on-site restaurant serves hearty French-leaning food, such as a mushroom, spinach, and Gruyère crêpe, *moules frites*, and duck confit.

Fitzrovia is also studded with pubs, including new bars that cater to recent arrivals from the media and art worlds. Mingle with locals at the Victorian-era Yorkshire Grey bar, festooned with BBC-related memorabilia—a nod to its location, a few blocks from the broadcasting studio. After work, the outside tables are filled with

Opposite, clockwise from top left: Foley Street; lamps at Heal's, on Tottenham Court Road; hailing a taxi on Goodge Street; books at French's Theatre Bookshop.

media and fashion types from nearby showrooms. Not far off and named after a defunct British department store where owner Mark Holdstock's mother once sold gloves, Bourne & Hollingsworth is a closet-size basement bar that is part 1920's speakeasy and part English tearoom, with floral wallpaper and killer retro cocktails (try the gin fizz or something from the innovative drinks list served Prohibition-style in teacups). The place is known for its monthly events, such as a swing music–powered Forties Blitz Party and gentlemen's etiquette classes on tie-knotting and martini-shaking. The low-lit, wood-paneled basement bar Shochu Lounge—designed by Japanese firm Super Potato—looks like a feudal *ryokan* reimagined by *Star Trek* set designers. It specializes in the Asian spirit *shochu*: try it mixed with plum-infused vodka in a Plum Plum. The bartender's Wylie Dufresne–like wizardry is also on show with blends such as a Bellini with pear-and-green-tea purée and a Hallo Kitty with rosewater, raspberries, and lemon juice. On the other end of the style spectrum, the classic Fitzroy Tavern is an ode to the 18th-century aristocrat Charles Fitzroy, for whom the neighborhood is said to be named. Until 1919 it was a café called the Hundred Marks, but once it morphed into a pub, it became the unofficial clubhouse of regulars such as Dylan Thomas, Nina Hamnett, and George Orwell.

Not surprisingly, most of the enclave's best shops cater to the artists and designers that now fill its streets. *The* place to find creative supplies in Fitzrovia, Alec Tiranti has been selling every material imaginable—clay, wax, rubber, glazes—as well as hardware, from kilns to modeling tools, since 1895. Beginners can peruse the hundreds of how-to books and videos alongside art-world heavy hitters. Drama buffs will want to visit the London outpost of the iconic New York publisher, French's Theatre Bookshop, to browse an encyclopedic selection of plays, both classic and contemporary. It's also a clearinghouse for underground theater events in the area—ask the knowledgeable staff or scan the poster-crammed notice board. You'll find a paper mecca of a different sort at the triple-decker site of the original Paperchase store, catering to artists in the area since the 1970's. On the first floor, look through a vast range of cards, Pop-arty boxes, and one-of-a-kind printed gift wrap. Then move upstairs for professional supplies—paper in various weights, day planners, and dozens of types of pens. The stately Heal's interiors

MUSICAL LIBRETTI

THE FITZROVIA No.1

Breakfast 10am-12
Monday to Saturday

store, which celebrated its 200th anniversary in 2010, is a British institution. Climb the stairs and check out the so-called Heal's cat, a sinewy 1925 sculpture by Chassagne peering from the mezzanine. The family began as bed makers, but in the mid-1890's, under fourth-generation chairman/designer Sir Ambrose Heal, the store expanded its offerings. It's still the perfect place for browsing the best in British design, from glassware and throw pillows to fabrics.

This flurry of commercial activity seems to belie Fitzrovia's reputation as a mostly residential area. Still, there's no shortage of great places to stay. Decorated like a chintz-filled country house that Bertie Wooster might share with Anya Hindmarch, the shabby-chic, 52-room Charlotte Street Hotel is filled with art curated by its co-owner, interior designer and collector Kit Kemp—from Roger Cecil abstracts to a contemporary mural by Alexander Hollweg. Like other Firmdale properties, it's known for its Sunday night film club, which combines dinner with a screening in the downstairs theater, complete with comfy leather loungers. The 380-room Langham (unveiled by the Prince of Wales in 1865 and a current royal favorite) recently underwent a $130

million renovation designed to restore some of its storied grandeur. Ceilings were raised, flat-screen TV's were added in all rooms, and a 50-foot underground pool was built in a former vault; in 2011, the Chuan Spa opened in the same space. Afternoon tea, British-style, is served daily in the Palm Court restaurant, reportedly where the tradition was born. Once a sleek furniture company headquarters nearby, the Sanderson became a hotel in 2000 under the guidance of Ian Schrager and Philippe Starck. The team preserved much of its Midcentury charm while adding signature touches (note the Daliesque red-lip sofa in the lobby). Suka, the Malaysian restaurant on site, was masterminded by New York's Zak Pelaccio, and the 300-square-foot guest rooms feel surprisingly large, with offbeat flourishes like a Starck-designed rug riffing on Voltaire's handwriting. The hotel's best amenity, though, is a well-kept secret: the Japanese-style Courtyard Garden hidden in the center of the building like an urban oasis. It features a lounge with a wooden deck set amid restored 1960's mosaics, rhododendrons, magnolias, and a man-made canal filled with white water lilies. But like the rest of Fitzrovia, it won't be a secret for long. ✚

Above, from left: The Langham hotel's Artesian bar; a painting by Antony Micallef, on display at Lazarides gallery. Opposite, from left: Utensils as artwork at Villandry restaurant; Bourne & Hollingsworth's manager Dino Koletsas.

resources

STAY

Charlotte Street Hotel
15 Charlotte St.; 44-20/7806-2000; firmdale.com; doubles from $$.

The Langham
1C Portland Place; 800/588-9141 or 44-20/7636-1000; langhamhotels.com; doubles from $$.

Sanderson 50 Berners St.; 800/697-1791 or 44-20/7300-1400; sandersonlondon.com; doubles from $$.

EAT

Benito's Hat
56 Goodge St.; 44-20/7637-3732; lunch for two ✗.

Lantana 13 Charlotte Place; 44-20/7637-3347; lunch for two ✗✗.

Salt Yard
54 Goodge St.; 44-20/7637-0657; dinner for two ✗✗.

Villandry 170 Great Portland St.; 44-20/7631-3131; dinner for two ✗✗✗.

DRINK

Bourne & Hollingsworth
28 Rathbone Place; 44-20/7636-8228; drinks for two ✗.

Fitzroy Tavern 16 Charlotte St.; 44-20/7580-3714; drinks for two ✗.

Shochu Lounge 37 Charlotte St.; 44-20/7580-6464; drinks for two ✗✗.

Yorkshire Grey 46 Langham St.; 44-20/7636-4788; drinks for two ✗.

GALLERIES

Alison Jacques Gallery
16-18 Berners St.; 44-20/7631-4720; alisonjacquesgallery.com.

Lazarides 11 Rathbone Place; 44-20/7636-5443; lazinc.com.

Pilar Corrias Gallery
54 Eastcastle St.; 44-20/7323-7000; pilarcorrias.com.

Stuart Shave/Modern Art
23-25 Eastcastle St.; 44-20/7299-7950; modernart.net.

SHOP

Alec Tiranti 27 Warren St.; 44-20/7380-0808; tiranti.co.uk.

French's Theatre Bookshop
52 Fitzroy St.; 44-20/7255-4300; samuelfrench-london.co.uk; closed on Sundays.

Heal's 196 Tottenham Court Rd.; 44-20/7636-1666; heals.co.uk.

Paperchase
213-215 Tottenham Court Rd.; 44-20/7467-6200; paperchase.co.uk.

ON THE STREET IN COPENHAGEN

In Denmark's environmentally minded capital, the bicycle is king. One popular thoroughfare: Højbro Plads, the 19th-century marketplace turned cosmopolitan crossroads at the center of Strøget, the city's first car-free zone. We asked 10 cyclists to stop and tell us where they were going, what not to miss, and what makes their hometown so appealing.

Vincent Byakika
Journalist

"When the sun shines, everyone heads to the green spaces, like Fælledparken in Østerport. If it snows, the city clears paths quickly, so you can ride all year. Today I visited **Nimb** *(5 Bernstorffsgade; 45/8870-0000; nimb.dk; doubles from $$$)*, a boutique hotel facing Tivoli. Now, I'm off to do some work at **Rayuela** *(5 Fælledvej; 45/3535-6674)*, a Spanish café and bookshop in Nørrebro."

Lars Danielsson
Musician

"The city's best live-music venue is **Vega** *(40 Enghavevej; 45/3325-7011)*, in Vesterbro. It was designed by Vilhelm Lauritzen, a renowned Danish architect. I also recommend **Copenhagen Jazzhouse** *(10 Niels Hemmingsens Gade; 45/3315-2600)* downtown, and in Nørrebro, there's **Rust** *(8 Guldbergsgade; 45/3524-5200)*, for up-and-comers."

Mille Dinesen
Actress

"Most Danish actors commute on bikes—even the famous ones. Sometimes my fans yell "Hi!" as I ride by. I like the shows at the **Royal Playhouse, Skuespilhuset** *(36 Sankt Annæ Plads; 45/3369-6933)*. After work, theater people go to **Viva** *(570 Langebrogade Kaj; 45/2725-0505)*, a restaurant and bar on a houseboat in Christianshavn."

Simon Grœnlund
Art Student

"My favorite museum is **Arken** *(100 Skovvej; 45/4354-0222; arken.dk)*, which has modern art. It's a 25-minute train ride from downtown, but the architecture alone—it looks like a stranded ship—is worth the trip. I also spend time around Studiestræde, a street with lots of cafés and secondhand shops."

Michaela Krigsager
Visual Culture Student

"The bicycles create a unique ambience. Here, there are three powerful visual velocities: cars, pedestrians, and cyclists. Most cities only have two. I like to go to the beach park at **Amager Strand** *(amager-strand.dk)*. You can see the windmills and the Oresund Bridge, so it has an industrial look. You have to take the train there, but I bring my bike on board."

Jacques Morild
Investment Banker

"Here, you can exercise and enjoy the surroundings while going about your business. I have a **Centurion** *(centurion.dk)*, a well-made Danish bike. I bought my hat at **Filippa K** *(various locations; filippa-k.com)*. On the weekends, I ride to Mindelunden i Ryvangen, a memorial park for the Danish World War II freedom fighters, in the suburb north of Copenhagen called Hellerup."

Vibeke and Giulio Castelli
Interior Decorator and Author

Vibeke: "I normally ride from the center of Copenhagen to Hellerup, past the Funkis houses; they are functionalist-minimalist, à la Arne Jacobsen." Giulio: "I spend a lot of time in the Black Diamond building at the **Royal Library** *(1 Søren Kierkegaards Plads; 45/3347-4747)*. It has concerts, exhibitions, and an excellent restaurant called **Søren K** *(45/3347-4949; dinner for two XXX)*, with seasonal cuisine."

Eva Skov Hansen
Doctor

"I visit my patients on a bike—I don't have to worry about parking a car. I like walking around the **Botanical Garden & Museum** *(130 Gothersgade; 45/3532-2222)*. The greenhouses were built in the 1800's by Carl Jacobsen, the father of Carlsberg beer. Microbreweries are popular here. My favorites are **Nørrebro Bryghus** *(3 Ryesgade; 45/3530-0530)* and **BrewPub** *(29 Vestergade; 45/3332-0060)*."

Lis Stahl
Great-grandmother

"I have always used a bicycle. My husband and I raised four children, and we never bought a car. During the war, the Germans took our gas, but they didn't take our bikes—we could still ride. I buy books at **Arnold Busck** *(49 Købmagergade; 45/3373-3500)* for my grandchildren and great-grandchildren."

Tilde Wolffbrandt
TV Producer

"Flexibility comes with using a bike. One of my favorite places to visit is the **Ny Carlsberg Glyptoteket** *(7 Dantes Plads; 45/3341-8141)*, a museum with a beautiful winter garden. It's best on Sundays, when admission is free. Right now I'm headed to the shop **Sneaky Fox** *(25A Studiestræde; 45/3391-2520)*, in the Latin Quarter. It's famous for colorful hosiery."

Clockwise from above: Vincent Byakika, a journalist; Lars Danielsson, a musician; actress Mille Dinesen; Simon Grœnlund, an art student; Michaela Krigsager, also a student; investment banker Jacques Morild; interior decorator Vibeke Castelli and her husband, author Giulio Castelli; doctor Eva Skov Hansen; Lis Stahl, a local great-grandmother. Near left: Television producer Tilde Wolffbrandt.

Memorial to the
Murdered Jews of
Europe, near the
Brandenburg Gate.

ADVENTURES
IN BERLIN

BY GARY SHTEYNGART
PHOTOGRAPHED BY MISCHA RICHTER

"**B**ERLIN IST GROSS UND ICH BIN KLEIN" (BERLIN IS BIG and I am small) reads a popular children's T-shirt featuring a forlorn mite of a penguin staring up at the immensity of East Berlin's iconic TV tower. At barely five foot six I know how that penguin feels. I have spent four months in Berlin talking to people's navels and having drinks passed over my head. If I ever joined the 13 percent of Berliners who are unemployed, I could make an attractive footstool for one of the gentle giants here. One night, at a bar in an outlying district, lost in a sea of blond heads crowned with halos of cheap smoke, I notice the kind of person who I think is still referred to as a midget waving happily to me across the room. I wave back with a big smile and an awkward thumbs-up. It is one of the happiest moments of my stay. I love the towering denizens of what is easily Europe's coolest metropolis. But now I know that I am not alone.

And there's more help on the way. Get out your measuring tape: the short, non-Teutonic folks are coming! By my estimate, at least half of them seem to be New York expatriates, intense, wiry, funny Jewish men who talk up their novel-in-progress, their nascent yoga practice, and their plans to open yet another art gallery to the interested local *Fräulein,* who peer down at them from their stratospheric heights. Making an absolute mockery of everything Joseph Goebbels ever stood for, Berlin is now a city where you hear more English than in New York and more Russian than in London. The foreigners come for the cheap rents, to be sure, but also for a nightlife that begins at midnight on Thursday and sputters dizzyingly to an end at 8 p.m. on Sunday. And there is so much culture that by the end of my stay I can only dream of using the bathroom of the neighborhood pub without running across a flyer touting a gallery opening, an avant-garde theater performance in a disused bathhouse, or the frightening advent of yet another "Bolshoi Bandits Russian Ska East Bloc Music DJ-Team Party." Berlin is its youth, and its youth are hip—even the teenage llama at the zoo has a fashionably retro Pat Benatar haircut. They are restless, and they are up for anything.

The new Berliners are one other thing: earnest. One of the greatest gifts that can fall in the lap of any emerging artist is the opportunity to fail. When you're paying 200 euros a month for a high-ceilinged room in a so-called W.G., or *Wohngemeinschaft,* an Oberlin-style "living community" where young people share chores and each other, you can spend years of your life "working only with adhesive tape," as one would-be Warhol told me. But maybe that's just the cynical New Yorker in me speaking. Whether German or foreign, these young people genuinely care about the communities they have forged out of the rubble of the 20th century's most problematic metropolis. And they appreciate the creative impulse around them, because it's still okay to be excited by things in Berlin.

To wit, a freezing Friday night in the middle of a season the rest of Europe still regards as autumn. At the Glass Pavilion of the Volksbühne theater in the former East, dozens of people are huddled together in the small space, warmed by nothing but cheap beer for free and the warbling of one overtaxed radiator. We are braving the elements to watch a brilliant short film by the British visual artist Tacita Dean about the British poet and translator Michael Hamburger, who was exiled from

Opposite: Inside Norman Foster's glass-and-steel Reichstag dome.

Bicycles parked in the bohemian neighborhood of Prenzlauer Berg.

Berlin in 1933 and passed away in 2007. The film flickers on the makeshift screen, the elderly poet is picking up apples and talking about them at great length ("I was very taken by the Devonshire…. It is just about the darkest apple I've ever seen"). The film is hypnotically simple and rendered with an ambient quality that somehow makes the end of life seem both close by and oddly matter-of-fact. As the film unfolds, there is not a sound in the little theater, except for the balding twenty- and thirtysomething men and very young women in vibrant leggings, who are taking snapshots of the screen with their cell phones. It's the kind of cultural encounter that I may pretend to remember from the New York of the 1980's and early 90's, but in any case it is here in Berlin *right now*—and it is touching and it is real.

My four months in the city were spent at the lakeside American Academy in Berlin (where I'd been invited to be a fellow for a semester). The Academy's villa is located in the near-distant suburb of Wannsee, across the lake from the House of the Wannsee Conference, where the Final Solution to the so-called Jewish Problem was signed. My temporary home had been owned by a Jewish banker who fled the country during the 1930's. The house then fell into the hands of the Third Reich's president of the Reichsbank, who added several architectural details, including my balcony. In the warmer months, I happened to divide my time between my Jewish study and my Nazi balcony (to add to the confusion, my bedroom was once occupied by the playwright Arthur Miller). Berlin, as the old adage from historian Karl

Scheffler goes, "is a city that never is, but is always in the process of becoming." The city the international art world has inherited has been in mad flux since the collapse of the Wall, but its physical infrastructure has more or less taken shape. Now that the terrific rupture of the Cold War has been sealed and partly cauterized, Berlin *has* become something—an often hypermodern, usually well-functioning, deindustrialized metropolis with almost no money. The results of the building boom have been uneven. The glass box of the chancellor's office has been rightly drubbed by locals as "the washing machine," while next door, the Reichstag, with its transparent Norman Foster dome and top-notch collection of contemporary art (cue Gerhard Richter's stunning interpretation of the German flag in the lobby), is a blessing upon the urban grid and a serious statement about Western democracy's chances of survival.

On the other hand, Potsdamer Platz, the new commercial and touristic heart of the city, resembles a rouged-up version of the skyline in Raleigh, North Carolina. Four billion dollars and five years were sunk into the building of this supposed future-scape just so that one of its main squares—Marlene-Dietrich-Platz, mind you—could host a McDonald's, a Starbucks, and a sad-looking casino. Arriving at the glassed-in Hauptbahnhof, the central train station that's one of the largest in Europe, is like pulling into a mall/office complex from the farthest reaches of suburbia. The task of reassembling a city whose history still has the capacity to make you gasp has led many of the world's best architects to perform open-heart surgery on Berlin's center, but along with generous helpings of glass and steel, they have injected a surfeit of anesthesia.

And yet, just a few minutes away from the studied plasticity of Potsdamer Platz lies the postwar Berliner Philharmonie, by architect Hans Scharoun—widely considered one of the best concert halls in the world and still the greatest artistic joy the city has to offer. The audience is seated like the U.N. General Assembly around the warm, glowing orchestra stage, and my favorite way to enjoy the music is not to close my eyes, but to remove my glasses and stare myopically at the golden haze around me, at the hushed and indistinct humanity; in this space, even the soft coughs of those afflicted by the city's damp air resound with a hidden melody. Conductor Simon Rattle's interpretation of Mahler's majestic and oddly hopeful Ninth Symphony brings the teenage concertgoer next to me to tears, and by the end of the performance she is shouting—*shouting*, mind you—for Sir Simon to grace us with an encore, which he does. How Berliners love their dandelion-haired British maestro.

AND THERE ARE MORE BERLINERS ON THE WAY. THE city is a baby-making machine. German parents receive a sizable subsidy for each child, and that child then collects a stipend until the age of 25. Hence, the tony eastern neighborhood of Prenzlauer Berg on a Thursday evening becomes a parade of well-dressed women on fancy bicycles with swaddled bundles of joy perched on the backseat, the occasional husband following behind at a respectful distance. The fecundity of these people is astonishing, and one wonders what this generation of new Berliners—born to be mild amid a landscape of hatha yoga and bio-products—will be like when it comes of age. While the children seem mellow, coddled, and rosy-cheeked, Berlin motherhood is fierce and competitive. Crossing at a red light while a *Kind* is watching might earn you the reproach "Are you color-blind?" from a mama worried that you are setting a dangerous example.

Trying to figure out Berlin's neighborhood of the moment is like trying to corner an especially smart chicken. But one thing is certain: the trend of colonizing the East in places like Prenzlauer Berg seems to have been reversed, with formerly uncool western neighborhoods that were the preserves of punks, draft dodgers, and the Turkish community during the Cold War—often beautiful Kreuzberg, but also the grittier Neukölln, to the south—now attracting the mommies and daddies of the city's creative class, not to mention a cascade of Americans with juicy Fulbrights.

My favorite stretch of Kreuzberg runs along the banks of the Landwehrkanal. Here, Turkish and bohemian Berlin meet in a way that makes the city feel as multicultural as Paris or London. On a Tuesday or a Friday I start at the Turkish Market, which stretches along the Maybachufer bank of the canal, to sample a smorgasbord of fat navel oranges, hot spinach *böreks* that flake to nothingness in your grasp, glowing aubergines, piles of octopus glistening in olive oil, every gradient of feta known to the Bosporus. The Anatolian young women in beautiful sequined chadors and men screaming out their prices until their voices break remind you of the greater world beyond the glacial forests and lakes of Brandenburg.

All that produce calls for a terrific meal. I head west along the canal to Defne, a restaurant that is nominally Turkish, but also smartly plays with the flavors of the Mediterranean. In other words, the greasy *döner* kebab that feeds Berlin's workers and party people is blessedly absent from the menu. One night I sit next to a German man with a beautiful flowing mullet like the mane of a balding lion, his breast adorned with a necklace of miniature pelts, perhaps an homage to the Navajo people. He is sampling one of my favorite dishes, the Imam Fainted—a zesty mix of eggplant with pine nuts and peppers, in a tomato-herb sauce. Defne also has the spiciest octopus in town, drowning in garlic and white-wine sauce and oven-baked with—I'm not really sure how this works—crumbly feta cheese. The so-called Well Brought Up Lamb skewer is charred but red-centered, and perfectly lives up to its name. Even more shocking, the service, for Berlin, is competent and caring: a waitress, when summoned, may come.

In need of a nightcap, I head to the nearby Ankerklause, a bar boat moored by the Turkish market, afloat with hipsters, punk rockers, and the occasional aging French tourist couple who have steered way off course. When the sun sets (that would be 5 p.m.), the bar becomes the kind of Berlin free-for-all that has made the city the world's capital of informality. As Johnny Cash's "Ring of Fire" blasts across the canal, I take a peek outside to watch the resident swans—those most blasé of Berliners—tuck their beaks beneath their wings and drift off to their complex avian dreams.

The swans are asleep, but the city is just getting started. Berlin *lives* by its nightlife. Even the average cabbie knows the score and will tell you that "Tresor is over and Café Moskau is full of teenagers," but Berghain is still the place to go. The club is housed in a muscular former power station in the gentrifying Friedrichshain area of the East, near the Spree River (you'll simply never find it). In its mix of straight and gay, this fantastically imposing space recaptures the Weimar aesthetic Berlin has been aching for ever since the Third Reich wiped out much of the city's eclectic culture. But before you can enter, a guy with three lip rings, some sort of pirate's vest, and the mien of a young Mozart—the bouncer, in other words—will carefully scrutinize your worth. "Berlin is *the* city for electronic dance music," says Mark Butler, a fellow at the American Academy and professor of music theory at Northwestern University, in Chicago, who has written extensively on the Berlin scene. "Almost every twenty- or thirtysomething you meet is a degree or two removed from someone who is recording techno or running a label." And half of them seem to convene at Berghain every Saturday night. By 9 a.m., when the club's shutters suddenly open to reveal the stealth arrival of a gray Berlin morning, the purist techno rhythms may well have grabbed your heart and taught it how to beat.

If not, something else will do the trick. Berlin may be tamer than it was in the 1990's, when people would organize spontaneous after-hour parties in the ATM vestibules of their local banks, but the nightlife is still thumping. Back in Kreuzberg, the Monarch bar, on the second floor of a hilariously dreary housing project, beckons the 40-year-old hipster who wishes to turn the clock back by exactly 15 years and is ready to groove to a disco version of "Hava Nagila" or the gypsy-punk band Gogol Bordello.

Wedding and Moabit are gentrifying neighborhoods of art galleries and new clubs just north of the Hauptbahnhof. Here is Haunch of Venison, a branch of the London gallery that put on a stunning display of Zhang Huan's 13-foot-tall *Berlin Buddha,* which was made entirely of incense ash and took three months to disintegrate—impermanence being yet another of this city's leitmotifs. Opposite the Haunch is a club called Tape, former home of the World Championship for Chess Boxing, where the contenders play chess for four minutes and then beat each other up. At other times, this enormous space hosts well-known acts like the Swiss diva Miss Kittin and the singer Peaches, the ever popular mistress of incorrectness, whose filthy Canadian mouth has found a perfect home in Berlin.

And then there's the Kosmetiksalon Babette, on the broad and unrepentantly socialist boulevard that is Karl-Marx-Allee, formerly known as Stalin Allee. The vodka martinis are excellent, and the bar's architecture alone is worth the visit—this former GDR cosmetics studio is an open constructivist glass box that would rank with the best of Warsaw Pact design. Glowing bright at night, its simplicity and inclusiveness belie its ridiculous roots.

As Berlin swells with expats, the question remains: Is this the new crucible of world culture or just an unusual city with a tiny airport? The galleries are here (although the buyers often are not), the nightlife, the youthful excitement, the coffee shops full of media types with laptops are all in evidence, but the international set

likes to eat well, and restaurants have never been Berlin's strong suit. That's changing. Celebrity chef Tim Raue, who did much for the city's cuisine at the restaurant 44 in the Swissôtel, has moved on from the famous Adlon Hotel to open Restaurant Tim Raue, in a former gallery in Kreuzberg. Here is a chef with the ability to bring Asian-chili heat to a humble piece of cod, a level of spicing appropriate for the global tongue. Another worthy entry is Facil, on the top floor of the Mandala Hotel at Potsdamer Platz. The space is reminiscent of the clean lines of the Neue Nationalgalerie down the street, and one is mesmerized by the two rows of chestnut trees—yellow and green in equal measure—shivering in the autumn cold on the attractive patio. The weird acoustics deposit snatches of political and economic German on your plate, along with the helicopter laughter of powerful men. The wine list is heavy on fine Austrian Sauvignon Blancs, and one night I was moved by a shoulder of Brandenburg venison with pine-cream chicory that was as good a treatment of the city's anorexic deer as I've ever had.

But this is above all a city of cozy neighborhoods—a local will swear foremost allegiance to his *Kiez*—and some of the best restaurants are little places that serve food, often from the south and west of Germany, to people from up and down the block. I'm thinking of a spot called Lebensmittel in Mitte, a grocery store with a shock of fresh green vegetables laid out in front, along with cans of tasty homemade cherry preserves. A typical night could find its back room full of nursing middle-aged mothers, their husbands dividing their time between the hollering tots and a soccer match on the television—as close as Berlin will ever get to feeling like Naples. Highlights include the occasional appetizer of lard with plums and bacon, a tender goose with a glistening layer of fat, and a plate of spaetzle egg noodles smothered with cheese and perfect for brunching.

A civilization can often be judged by the quality of its chicken, and Kreuzberg's legendary Henne offers the moistest, crispiest milk-roasted bird to be found in *Mitteleuropa,* along with a décor that's a celebration of Berlin as a working-class city, with its wooden ceilings, tartan tablecloths, and nicotine-stained walls. A draught of golden *Landbier* from the northern part of Bavaria and the occasional drag of a forbidden cigarette (Berlin has enacted a shocking smoking ban) will help you feel as drunk and rheumatic as the rest of the clientele.

Opposite, clockwise from top left: The Kaiser Wilhelm Memorial Church, on Breitscheidplatz, the center of former West Berlin; the Potsdamer Platz train station, including graffiti-covered remnants of the Wall; shoppers at the Turkish Market, on the edge of Kreuzberg; Henne's copper beer taps.

Opposite:
Paul-Löbe-Haus,
near the
Reichstag.

In another part of Kreuzberg, on the relatively posh Bergmannstrasse, I swear by the restaurant Austria, which I love for more than its monstrously sized schnitzel perched atop a tangy potato salad made with onion and vinegar. In this folksy, low-ceilinged, crimson setting, former Berlin resident Jeffrey Eugenides celebrated the completion of one of the best novels of the new century, the Pulitzer Prize–winning *Middlesex*. In fact, the hero(ine) of his novel goes on an important date here and is taken with the deer antlers that line the restaurant's walls. During my last meal at Austria, I watch yet another young Berlin mother cutting a schnitzel with an optician's precision for her brood of three. Two children are reaching up for the crusty bits of veal like newborn chicks, but one little fellow is too engrossed to eat: he is… *reading a book*. "The restaurant is dark, warm, woody and comfortable," Eugenides writes. "Anybody who wouldn't like it is somebody I wouldn't like."

One chilly morning, after consuming our body weight in schnitzel, a short Jewish friend and I cross the lake to the House of the Wannsee Conference, where on January 20, 1942, the head of the Reich Security Main Office, Reinhard Heydrich, invited a group of gentlemen for "a meeting to be followed by breakfast." The gentlemen in question were high-ranking members of the S.S. and other Nazi entities; the meeting was a plan to murder all European Jews; and the breakfast must have been a traditionally healthy German one, with lots of small talk and gales of morning laughter. As with all German historical sites, the documentation in this thoroughly pleasant lakeside villa is meticulous. After learning of the Nazi plan to deport the country's Jews to Madagascar (if only!), my friend and I realize that most of the conference involved the so-called *Mischling* question—in other words, what to do with Germans of mixed Jewish-Aryan blood. After deliberating the semantics of the question for an hour and a half, the gentlemen decided that if an individual looks, "feels, and behaves" like a Jew, then he "should be classed with the Jews"—in other words, gassed. As I'm stroking my dense, near-rabbinical beard and my friend is playing with her Sephardic curls, the inevitable older German woman quickly gravitates to us and says, apologetically, "It was a dark time in our history." And I'm torn between sadness and revulsion, an appreciation of the sentiment, and the impotent feeling that I do not have the power to absolve.

THE VISUAL ARTIST THOMAS DEMAND IS, IN MY opinion, the finest artist in Germany today. Some of his work re-creates life-size models of recent historical events—for example, the lectern used by Serbian dictator Slobodan Milošević in 1989 to declare open season on Yugoslavia's other ethnic groups (*Podium*). The models, constructed of colored paper and cardboard, are photographed and then destroyed. Whatever the subject matter, these works, to my mind, accurately and honestly capture what it means to be born under the canopy of history in a perennially overcast part of the world. Demand is able to tease out a paper-thin beauty from his often mundane subjects, while in a work like *Podium* we are left with a brief, if stylized, portrait of what history looks like during the tremulous instant, that last exhale of breath, before the slaughter begins. Which is to say that unlike that of other contemporary artists, Demand's vision frightens me. He works from a 15,000-square-foot storage building behind the Hamburger Bahnhof museum, a place that in any other "world city" would house 800 graphic designers and an overpriced Thai-Mexican restaurant. Part of Demand's factory space is cantilevered over a garden that used to be taken up with train tracks, a potent Berlin symbol, while his studio building runs right up to the frontier of the former Berlin Wall. "Can't do anything about it," Demand says, one finger on his thick dark frames. "History is everywhere."

He's right. Even today, Berlin's guilt infrastructure is almost completely in place. Tributes to its tragic past continue to crop up, including the thousands of concrete slabs that form the Memorial to the Murdered Jews of Europe, a stone's throw from the Brandenburg Gate and the new U.S. Embassy. The most impressive memorial, however, does not aspire to architectural glory or to strenuous interpretation. I take the S-Bahn west for 20 minutes to the tiny suburban train station of quiet, leafy Grunewald. Between 1941 and 1945, more than 55,000 Jewish Berliners were deported to extermination camps from what is now a disused track labeled Gleis 17. The dates of deportation and the destinations of the trains are carved onto the edge of the platform. But on the day I come to the memorial, my last day in Berlin, a fresh snow has obscured everything. Only the lights of nearby cottages blink in the gloom. And all I can see are snow-covered boughs gently arching across the tracks. And there, in the far distance, some young trees, sturdy and short, have found a foothold. ✚

resources

STAY

Art'Otel
85 Lietzenburgerstrasse,
Wilmersdorf; 49-30/887-7770;
artotel.de; doubles from $.

**Kempinski Hotel Bristol
Berlin** 27 Kurfürstendamm,
Wilmersdorf; 800/426-
3135 or 49-30/884-340;
kempinski-berlin.de;
doubles from $.

Ritz-Carlton, Berlin
3 Potsdamer Platz,
Tiergarten; 800/241-3333 or
49-30/337-777; ritzcarlton.
com; doubles from $$.

EAT

Austria 30 Bergmannstrasse,
Kreuzberg; 49-30/694-4440;
dinner for two ✖✖.

Defne Restaurant 92C Planufer,
Kreuzberg; 49-30/8179-7111;
dinner for two ✖✖.

Facil 3 Potsdamer Str.,
Tiergarten; 49-30/59-005-
1234; dinner for two ✖✖✖✖.

Henne 25 Leuschnerdamm,
Kreuzberg; 49-30/614-7730;
dinner for two ✖✖.

Lebensmittel in Mitte
2 Rochstrasse, Mitte; 49-
30/2759-6130; lunch for two ✖.

DRINK

Ankerklause 104 Kottbusser
Damm, Kreuzberg; 49-30/693-
5649; drinks for two ✖.

Berghain Am Wriezener
Bahnhof, Friedrichshain; no
phone; berghain.de; drinks
for two ✖.

Kosmetiksalon Babette
36 Karl-Marx-Allee,
Friedrichshain; no phone;
drinks for two ✖.

Monarch 134 Skalitzer Str.,
Kreuzberg; no phone; drinks
for two ✖.

Tape 14 Heidestrasse, Moabit;
49-30/2848-4873; drinks for
two ✖.

DO

American Academy in Berlin
17-19 Am Sandwerder,
Wannsee; 49-30/804-830;
americanacademy.de.

Berliner Philharmonie
1 Herbert-von-Karajan-Strasse,
Tiergarten; 49-30/254-880;
berliner-philharmoniker.de.

Gleis 17 Memorial Grunewald;
no phone; gleis-17.de.

**Haunch of Venison
Berlin** 46 Heidestrasse,
Moabit; 49-30/3974-3963;
haunchofvenison.com.

**House of the Wannsee
Conference** 56-58 Am
Grossen Wannsee, Wannsee;
49-30/805-0010; ghwk.de.

**Kaiser Wilhelm Memorial
Church** Breitscheidplatz,
Charlottenberg.

**Memorial to the Murdered
Jews of Europe** 1 Cora-
Berliner-Strasse, Mitte;
49-30/2639-4336;
stiftung-denkmal.de.

Reichstag Platz der Republik.
Tiergarten; 49-30/2270;
bundestag.de.

Turkish Market
Maybachufer, Neukölln.

Swimming at
Le Mas des Lauriers, in
Puyricard, France.

quiet retreats

THE ART OF THE ENGLISH GARDEN

BY DOMINIQUE BROWNING

PHOTOGRAPHED BY SIMON BROWN

Looking across the Long Border to the 15th-century main house at Great Dixter Gardens, in Northiam, England. Opposite: A row of lupines.

WHEN WE FINALLY DO GET INSIDE, ON THAT FIRST wintry morning, it is to gather at an enormous hearth whose opening is nearly as tall as I am; large, perfectly seasoned logs are stacked beside it. The blazing fire warms the vast room. At Dixter, house and garden are equally impressive. Both were designed for Christo's parents in 1910 by the renowned architect Edwin Lutyens, who had earned a reputation for making old houses sing. He worked in collaboration with garden designer Gertrude Jekyll, though Christo's father, Nathaniel, and his mother, Daisy, were hands-on gardeners and designers.

Life in the house continues to follow the same patterns laid down decades ago: cocktails include Christo's favorite 12-year-old Scotch, Syndicate; every evening, our dinner is prepared by the genial manager of house and garden, Aaron Bertelsen, who uses the same handwritten recipes that Daisy served her guests a hundred years earlier. The house is so well-loved and so full of living that I half expect Christo himself to join us for a cocktail.

We take ours during a lecture called "Tools of the Trade." That may sound rather basic, but even experienced gardeners come upon things they have never seen before. (Luckily, the Dixter gift shop has a treasure trove of unusual, distinctive offerings.) Garrett demonstrates the proper way to divide the root ball of a perennial, plunging two forks, back to back, into the tangle and gently but firmly thrusting them apart. The "tickling fork," with its long handle and stubby fingers, ideal for fluffing the soil after planting, turns out to be a group favorite. I order one immediately.

We move into the billiard room for the first of several slideshows that will introduce us to the gardens. We get a vivid picture of the various mixed borders full of trees, shrubs, perennials, biannuals, and annuals; Dixter's gardens are models of "succession planting," in which beds are constantly added to throughout the growing season as flowers are spent and plants go dormant. Garrett points out which plants are self-sowers, popping up wherever their seeds have drifted; he shows us how climbing plants such as clematis and some roses are encouraged to clamber through the larger shrubs and trees. He asks us to pay attention to the contrasting shapes and textures of plants, noting how there is a good undulation in their heights. The colors of the garden in full summer are inebriating. "But turn these pictures into black and white," Garrett emphasizes, "and the compositions still work."

Garrett tells stories about his early days at Dixter, how Christo would move about with his notebook, recording color combinations, heights of plants, their fragrance, the health of the beds. He wrote a weekly column for *Country Life* for an astonishing 42 years. "But there was always laughter in the garden," Garrett says. "'You've got to enjoy it,' he would tell the young people working with him." Christo taught Garrett that gardening was like painting a picture, one that changed every month. "Dixter is all about spirit—and atmosphere," he says.

On the morning of our second lecture, "The Basics of Soil Composition," we are ushered into the Great Hall, where the fire is again roaring. Nearly 40 plates of compost and various types and components of soil have been laid out in rows on the floor. We are encouraged to grab fistfuls of the materials, squeeze them, sniff them. Soil with a healthy tilth actually smells delicious.

The rich soil is perfect for the flower beds; the meadows, on the other hand, need to be starved for the plants to thrive. There, the topsoil is very thin, and cuttings are raked off when the grounds are mowed. Stress is good for meadows—and Dixter's meadows, in spring and summer, are spangled with the jewel colors of fritillarias, orchids, crocus, primroses, daisies, violets. Some visitors to Dixter have been known to complain that it looks as though the mowing hasn't been completed. But Garrett defends the meadows as not only a beautiful addition that softens the strong lines of the paths and beds but also as being important for biodiversity. "Ninety-five percent of species-rich lowland meadows have disappeared in the U.K. since World War II," he explains.

"The main thing is not to plant against nature," Garrett says when he realizes his students are straining to understand the chemistry of keeping soil in balance. "But if you are starting a new garden, you may have to break the back of your soil. Cart it out and redo it, even if you have to delay planting for a year or two." I think ruefully of the heavy clay in my garden. I had been in a rush to start planting when the construction around my house was finally done. Now I pay for that impatience every time I put a spade into the ground. I'll be forever trying to catch up on enriching it.

Garrett has organized several field trips for our group. We visit the world's preeminent breeder of hamamelis (witch hazel) and are dazzled by the variety of reds, yellows, ochers, and oranges covering every branch of hundreds of shrubs. We motor over to nearby Sissinghurst Castle, whose famous white flower beds are just being cleaned for spring. One evening, the country's best dahlia propagator visits and gives us a lecture about the obsessive discipline needed to cultivate showstopping blossoms for competition.

Christo wanted to train future generations of gardeners, and Garrett has taken up that important work. I am again struck by how seriously the English take their gardening,

how people train for years to be able to take over the management of large public and private places, and how often the love of gardens is passed down from one generation to the next. Garrett remarks that it is getting harder to find young people who want to make gardens their livelihood, yet there is no end of volunteers who are willing to trade room and board at Dixter for a few months of the best hands-on training they could ever get.

Time is suspended at Great Dixter. To spend a week gardening there is to enter a magical dimension in a nurturing place, grounded in rich legacy, enthralling beauty, and the bright companionability of growing flowers and sharing them with the world. Dixter is a place that shows you how a garden can be the work of a lifetime, and how a lifetime can be immeasurably enhanced by coursing along with the rhythms of the seasons. It is a place where everything, from the hangings over the hearth to the piling of the compost, is the seamless expression of an interesting, quirky sensibility—one that will continue to enchant, inspire, and instruct generations of guests.

Over the next several days, we tromp in and out of the garden, layering on waterproof pants and jackets, bundling up in scarves and hats. We are assigned the task of pruning the large shrubs and small trees dotted through the mixed borders, as Garrett looks on. "Strong will give rise to strong," he reminds us. "Plants that flower on new growth should be pruned in late winter. Plants that flower on old growth should be pruned after blooming. But we want you to learn to think for yourself. Just look at the plant, and figure it out. What does it want?" His voice will stay with me for months after I return to my own garden. ✚

resources

Many of England's top gardens are open to the public for tours. Here are some of our favorites.

Alnwick Garden
Restored complex of formal gardens with lots of child-friendly activities. Alnwick, Northumberland; 44-1665/511-350; alnwickgarden.com.

Beth Chatto Gardens
Eco-gardeners Beth and Andrew Chatto restored this once-barren land; each month the garden holds one-day workshops on site. Colchester, Essex; 44-1206/822-007; bethchatto.co.uk.

Great Dixter House & Gardens
Northiam, East Sussex; 44-1797/252-878; greatdixter.

co.uk; open April–October; weeklong symposia from $$$$$ per person, including meals and lodging.

Hidcote Manor Garden
Famous for its enchanting outdoor "rooms" designed by naturalist and exotic-plant hunter Major Lawrence Johnston. Hidcote Bartrim, Gloucestershire; 44-1386/

438-333; nationaltrust.org.uk; open March–December.

Sissinghurst Castle Garden
Created by Bloomsbury habitué Vita Sackville-West in 1930; renowned for its roses and striking White Garden. Cranbrook, Kent; 44-1580/710-701; nationaltrust.org.uk; open March–October.

SPOTLIGHT
SECRET VILLAGES

No traffic jams, no Internet cafés, and no crowds—just centuries-old charm
and an authentic way of life. That's what you'll find
in these five hidden spots across Europe where time stands still.

Norcia, Italy

In this Umbrian citadel 69 miles northeast of Rome, artisanal culinary traditions endure. Pecorino cheese is aged for two years, honey is sourced from the wildflowers that bloom in the plains, and trained dogs sniff out black truffles in the woodlands. Sample them with strangozzi pasta at **Il Granaro del Monte** *(6 Via Alfieri; 39-0743/816-513; dinner for two* **XXX***)*. But it's the *cinghiale* (wild boar) that takes pride of place. Ask any of the shopkeepers in the *centro storico* to slice up fresh *ciauscoli*, spiced wild-boar salumi cured with methods perfected over 800 years, and bring it to the Piazza San

STAUFEN IM BREISGAU, GERMANY

HALL IN TIROL, AUSTRIA

CHASSIGNOLLES, FRANCE

NORCIA, ITALY

MARVÃO, PORTUGAL

Clockwise from left: The bar at France's Auberge de Chassignolles; a serving of its apple-and-elderberry crumble with custard ice cream; looking toward Chassignolles' 12th-century church; the Piazza San Benedetto, in Norcia, Italy; an Auberge de Chassignolles sheep; the Moorish castle that dominates Marvão, Portugal; a quiet street in Staufen im Breisgau, Germany; a dish from Alfred Schladerer, in Staufen; an employee at Alfred Schladerer; a scenic corner of Hall in Tirol, Austria.

Benedetto. Stay at the 24-room **Palazzo Seneca** *(12 Via Cesare Battisti; 39-0743/817-434; palazzo seneca.com; doubles from $)*, set in a 16th-century palace.

Staufen im Breisgau, Germany

Driving south from Strasbourg, you'll pass hills covered with terraced vineyards en route to this wine-lover's enclave on the edge of the Black Forest. Main Street's pastel houses lead to the Gothic marketplace and Town Hall; join the businessmen at the outdoor wine bar or pick up a bottle of plum eau-de-vie at **Alfred Schladerer** *(1 Alfred-Schladerer-Platz; 49-76/338-320; schladerer.de)*, a distillery run by vintners Heiner Ulmann and Philipp Schladerer. Retreat to one of 12 patterned rooms at **Hotel-Gasthof Kreuz-Post** *(65 Hauptstrasse; 49-76/339-5320; kreuz-post-staufen.de; doubles from $)*. Overindulgers beware: legend has it that any reveler who falls into one of the town's (sparkling-clean) irrigation ditches is destined to marry a local.

Chassignolles, France

Popular with Marseilles' elite in the 1950's, Chassignolles promises rolling hills studded with dormant green volcanoes and winding streams purported to have healing qualities. Use the **Auberge de Chassignolles** *(Le Bourg; 33-4/71-76-32-36; aubergedechassignolles.com; doubles from $; dinner for two ✗✗)*—a 1930's-era stone inn that looks out toward a 12th-century Romanesque church—as your base. The chefs at the auberge will pack you a picnic basket for the meandering, 90-minute walk to Durbiat, an even smaller village with a crumbling castle. Just be sure to get back in time for dinner at the hotel's restaurant, which serves an ever-changing menu of Auvergne specialties such as *pounti*—a pork, Swiss-chard, and prune tartine—and *tarte aux cèpes*.

Marvão, Portugal

Marvão is the king of mountainside forts. Located in the southeastern Alentejo region, near Lisbon, the whitewashed town is centered around a Moorish castle that was Christianized in the 13th century. The stone complex, now laid open to the elements in a kind of tumbledown glory, sits atop a rocky hill, dominating the town and its red-tile-roofed houses and convents. Check in to the **Pousada Santa Maria** *(7 Rua 24 de Janeiro; 351/245-993-201; pousadas.pt; doubles from $)*, a simple 31-room hotel and restaurant constructed from a foundry and two 13th-century houses. Fill up on

goat casserole at the lunch counter of the open-air **Varanda do Alentejo** *(1 Praça do Pelhourinho; 351/245-993-272; lunch for two ✗✗)*.

Hall in Tirol, Austria

Take a 10-minute commuter train from Innsbruck straight into what feels like the Middle Ages. Hall in Tirol, established in 1303, has remained unusually intact thanks to the medieval embankment and the area's wealth from salt mining and minting. But the town's allure comes from its surroundings: the Alps, with hiking and ski trails galore. Stay at the **Goldener Engl** *(5 Unterer Stadtplatz; 43-5223/54621; goldener-engl.at; doubles from $)*, whose rooms balance stately grandeur with Alpine kitsch. Enjoy the après-ski scene at **Pipistrello** *(22 Stadtgraben; 43-699/1220-9191; drinks for two ✗)*, a wine and schnapps bar.

AT HOME
IN PROVENCE

BY LUKE BARR
PHOTOGRAPHED BY MAX KIM-BEE

The courtyard at Le Mas des Lauriers, the farmhouse the author's family rented on the outskirts of Aix-en-Provence. Opposite: Figs at the Place Richelme farmers' market, in Aix.

We

SHOPPED MORNING, NOON, AND night in Provence—we shopped for croissants, baguettes, newspapers, and cigarettes, for tomatoes, peaches, string beans, strawberries, eggplants, mushrooms, and lettuce. We shopped for legs of lamb and chickens, for cubes of beef for stew, and for pork sausages. We shopped for butter and milk and cheese, and for honey and cases of wine and Badoit mineral water. We shopped for breakfast, lunch, and dinner, and then we started over again.

For basic provisions, we went into the village—our house was in tiny Puyricard, on the outskirts of Aix. The town had an old stone church next to the post office, three bakeries, a little Casino supermarket, a butcher, and a café with vaguely unfriendly, pastis-drinking middle-aged men, the kind that can be found in every French village. Sometimes they played *pétanque*.

I never did figure out which bakery had the best croissants, and it didn't matter—they were all good. We bought them eight or 10 at a time: not too big, buttery but not overly rich, satisfyingly crunchy but still tender and elastic inside. At the newsstand we'd pick up the *International Herald Tribune* and *L'Équipe*, the sports tabloid. We got to know the mom, pop, and son who ran the supermarket and who did their best to help find what we needed, with mixed success (dried red-pepper flakes? "...*Non*," came the reply, heads shaking sadly). The butcher was hip and friendly, in his thirties but his close-cropped hair already going gray. His lamb chops were incredible.

And so it was that we developed a routine, a rhythm, a kind of easygoing daily schedule, loosely correlated to hunger and appetite. The main event was the farmers' market in downtown Aix. On the Place Richelme, in the shade of a canopy of tall plane trees, this was a farmers' market to end all farmers' markets. Not that it was very big, or particularly fancy, but it was idyllic; the market was busy from early morning until just after lunch, full of sturdy matrons pulling two-wheeled carts and parents pushing strollers. The vegetables were beautiful—densely colored peppers and tomatoes, fresh garlic—and the fruits were even more beautiful—small, sweet strawberries; baskets of red currants, figs, and apricots; all sorts of peaches, nectarines, plums, and melons. One man sold goat cheeses, aged to different vintages, and honey; another had hams and salami, including a heavy and rectangular aged *lonzo* from Corsica. We sliced our pieces thin, so it would last longer.

I have every reason to love the market in the Place Richelme: I inherited a love for it—indeed, for Aix itself. My father lived here when he was a kid in 1959: my grandmother, Norah Barr, brought her three sons and rented a house not far from her sister, M.F.K. Fisher, who had rented a place just outside Aix with her two daughters. I grew up hearing about this epic trip, and an earlier one in 1954—from my father and uncles, mostly, about the boat ride from California down

Opposite, clockwise from top left: Vegetable stands at Aix's farmers' market; salami for sale; the Cours Mirabeau, the town's main boulevard; freshly made chèvre.

through the Panama Canal and across the Atlantic; about learning French in school in Switzerland and then moving to France for the other half of the year, attending the same lycée Paul Cézanne had; about how my dad, at age 13, was able to distinguish the white wines of Switzerland by town of origin; about how they all rode around on Solex motorbikes and read Tintin comics.

M.F. by this point was a well-established writer, and she recorded the trip in subsequent years—in 1964 in *Map of Another Town*, for example, a book about Aix. She described the "green light" that filtered through the plane trees above the market at Place Richelme in an essay for *The New Yorker* in 1966: "Perhaps some fortunate fish have known it, but for human beings it is rare to float at the bottom of the deeps and yet breathe with rapture the smells of all the living things spread out to sell in the pure, filtered, moving air."

Rereading her today, it's often striking how little has changed. Fifty years later, the market is precisely as she described it, minus the "ducklings bright-eyed in their crates" and other livestock. Then again, in many other ways Aix has also changed completely—and so what if it has? I'm not going to pretend to be nostalgic about 1959—hell, I was born in 1968. But on this trip I was accompanied by my father and my grandmother, and I did want to see the city through their eyes—however momentarily, in whatever glancing, refracted way, to have a visceral sense of a past that lives on embedded in the present. But the strange thing is that's not what happened at all. Or at least not the only thing.

THE HOUSE WE RENTED CAME WITH A RABBIT, AND of course the kids loved him. He was plump and brown, and lived in a rather elegant wood-and-stone–framed cage underneath the fig tree. We fed him carrots, and joked about eating him for dinner.

Our bedrooms were on the second floor of the 300-year-old *mas*, a solidly constructed stone building covered in vines and with terra-cotta-tiled floors. The kitchen was simple and spare, and had a long, zinc-topped table at its center and a door that opened out onto the graveled courtyard. In the morning I would walk out, say hello to the rabbit, and sit on one of the rickety chairs at the rickety wood-slat table, or on a creaking canvas lounge chair under the enormous plane tree, and drink my coffee. Who was driving into town, and how many baguettes did we need?

In addition to my grandmother and father, our group included my wife and daughter, and my childhood friend Adrian and his wife and son. The kids were both four, and spent half the time in the pool. We also had a stream of friends passing through—on the way back to Zurich from Spain, or on the way to Paris, or on vacation from New York. Our visitors stayed in the guest cottage, an adorable, slightly dilapidated little house out in the garden.

The grounds were magnificent: sprawling lawns; olive, apple, plum, fig, and unruly cypress trees; lavender and rosemary bushes all over—the lavender positively thrumming with bees—white and dark pink laurel, grapevines, and potted lemon trees; a *pétanque* court, a ping-pong table, a fabulous and overgrown herb garden—dry, fragrant thyme and sage, basil, lemon verbena, and three varieties of rosemary; a pristine pool and a pool house with a chimneyed charcoal grill and a large dining table.

We ate all our meals outside, carrying the heavy glasses, dishes, and silverware to the table in shallow wicker baskets. We ate tomatoes drizzled with olive oil, vinegar, and chopped fresh herbs at every opportunity. We grilled many lamb chops, marinated in lemon juice, olive oil, rosemary, thyme, and garlic, and made potato gratins with Gruyère, and gnocchi with butter and sage, and my grandmother's awe-inspiring ratatouille.

Some combination of the dry heat and the easy back-and-forth from inside to outside—the screenless doors and windows were always open, with warm breezes, children, and the occasional grasshopper making their way in and out of the house—reminded me of California. My grandmother's house in Sonoma, the house I grew up loving, had a similarly overgrown and carelessly beautiful garden, a row of tall poplar trees, a scruffy lawn, and flower and vegetable plantings overlooking the Russian River and the Pacific Ocean. Inside were cats and a dog, threadbare Oriental carpets, a large kitchen, and endless evening bridge games. M.F.'s house in Glen Ellen was a little more formal, a thick-walled palazzo set back from the road overlooking a field of grapevines, but both of them epitomized for me a sort of genteel, unpretentious, and yet highly sophisticated California style.

I always knew, of course, that our California life had a Provençal flavor, in the dishes my grandmother and

great-aunt cooked, in the art hung on their walls. But it wasn't until I arrived that I really understood how much of my family's aesthetic and cultural DNA had its roots right here, in Aix.

Aix is a university town and former provincial capital, built around Roman baths and numerous churches. It has narrow cobblestoned streets leading through various plazas, and it's built on a slope. And so the town seems to carry you gently but persuasively down the hill and toward its center, at least when you enter, as we did, from the north side, which was where the road from Puyricard deposited us. The streets were lined with clothing stores, cafés, gift shops, and patisseries. One day my wife and I stopped to buy some Provençal dishes to replace the ones my grandmother bought back in the 1950's and 60's and which I still used (they ended up in my kitchen a few years back), even though they were chipped and quite possibly full of lead, i.e., poisonous. The dishes at Soulèo Provence were almost identical to the ones we had, beautiful medium yellows and dark greens, and the salesman assured me that they did indeed at one time have "the maximum amount of lead,"

but no longer. We bought as many plates and bowls as seemed reasonable to carry.

As I say, the town pulls you toward its heart, its grand central street, the Cours Mirabeau. With two tall rows of plane trees and a series of fountains and cafés, it makes you slow down and exhale. M.F. described the Cours this way: "It is a man-made miracle, perhaps indescribable, compounded of stone and water and trees, and to the fortunate it is one of the world's chosen spots for their own sentient growth." I'm not sure I experienced "sentient growth," but I wholeheartedly agree.

We ate dinner at Les Deux Garçons, the famous (and these days quite touristy) café on the Cours, a place where M.F. spent hours watching the comings and goings, and never a place one came for the food, but rather for the ambience, as my grandmother pointed out. My daughter ordered a hamburger, and was of course dismayed when it failed to arrive with a bun. She soon managed to polish it off, however.

Not far away, on a quiet street just off the Cours, we paid a visit—we paid our respects, I want to say—to the fountain of the Four Dolphins. This fountain was

Above, from left: The kitchen at La Pitchoune, Julia Child's onetime house in Plascassier; cafés along the Cours Mirabeau.

Above, from left: Boats docked harborside in Cassis; La Grande Plage. Opposite, from left: The terrace at L'Hostellerie de l'Abbaye de la Celle, a restaurant 45 minutes from Aix; Rue Cardinale, in Aix, with a view of the Église St.-Jean de Malte.

my grandmother and M.F.'s favorite, my father and his brothers and cousins' favorite: our family favorite, in other words. As advertised, the fountain consisted of four stone dolphins, smiling and cheerful but each with a slightly different expression, spouting thin streams of water into the basin below. "This fountain is great," said my father definitively, expressing neither a strictly aesthetic judgment nor simple, unbridled enthusiasm, but rather something more transcendent, a serious claim of affection, and one that he wanted us to share. He remembered the Four Dolphins so well from when he was 13, and here it was, some 50 years later, and still wonderful.

But of course, some things do not survive, some things become unrecognizable. A few blocks away was the Hôtel Roi René, where we now thought we'd go for an after-dinner drink before heading back to the house. The Roi René was once *the* hotel in Aix, the epitome of elegance and so forth, the place where M.F. had stayed for weeks at a time in the early 50's, where she and my grandmother and the kids would check in every so often for a weekend in the late 50's, to take hot baths and order room service, and where my father remembers a sprawling suite with

a balcony overlooking the Boulevard du Roi René, and watching the Tour de France whiz by below.

As we walked in we were confronted with a beige-and-pink color scheme and a collection of hyperbanal corporate furniture. The place had none of the glamour my dad and grandmother remembered—not an iota.

My father looked puzzled, studying the angles of the walls and wondering if the original hotel had been torn down and completely rebuilt. No, he and my grandmother decided, but significant structural changes had been made at some point or other. We were directed to a table with a view of the inner courtyard.

"Well, too bad," my grandmother said.

Yup, I said. But we might as well have a drink, right?

Sure, everyone agreed. We looked around for a few minutes at the perfectly pleasant and yet perfectly uninspiring hotel lobby.

After a while, no waiter had appeared.

Well, I said, I guess we may as well leave, right? Everyone agreed, and we quickly departed.

There was plenty of time, over the course of a lazy two weeks in July, for a few road trips. One day we drove

to Cassis, about 45 minutes away on the Mediterranean. We wanted to swim at a beach, in the waves and among the sandy crowds. The coastline here was nothing if not dramatic, the drive down into town a series of steep switchbacks, the blue expanse of the ocean floating in the mid-distance like a dream. The town itself was charming and picturesque in the way that only a fishing village can be—with narrow streets and dockside restaurants, cliffs looming in the background and a blazing sun overhead. We sprang for the 15-euro-a-day chaise longues and beach umbrellas, and watched the kids splash around in the surf. Every 45 minutes or so I would dive into the water to cool off, floating on my back and staring at the sky.

Another day, we made our way to L'Hostellerie de l'Abbaye de la Celle, a small country inn and restaurant owned by Alain Ducasse, for a long afternoon lunch. La Celle is a tiny village about 45 minutes from Aix, and the inn incorporates a former Benedictine abbey, a 12th-century building that extends on one side of a back courtyard, where tables are set on the terrace under large canvas umbrellas. We ordered prix fixe tasting

menus in the absolutely serene garden: artichoke hearts and mushroom ravioli, red mullet with tomato, basil, and balsamic reduction, veal loin roasted with sage, and so on and so forth.

A far less elaborate meal awaited us at La Pitchoune, Julia and Paul Child's onetime house near Plascassier, 95 miles east of Aix. This was the vacation house Julia built on Simone Beck's family estate in 1962, a place where she cooked and entertained. Today it's home to Cooking with Friends in France, a culinary immersion program run by Kathie Alex, a former student of Beck's. The kitchen is as Julia left it, with the outlines of her utensils stenciled on the Peg-Board wall.

We sat with Alex on the terrace eating *salade niçoise* next to a small olive tree, looking out over the craggy landscape. My grandmother and M.F. had been here in 1970, a moment when the entire American culinary establishment seems to have arrived en masse in the immediate area—in addition to the Childs, James Beard, Bert Greene, Richard Olney, Judith and Evan Jones, all cooking, eating, and writing. They were pioneers of taste, but also of having taste, of cooking and "the art of eating," bringing European recipes and attitudes to an American audience.

I loved the gravel in Provence: the sound of it under the wheels of the car in the potholed driveway, the expanse of it around our house, on the paths to the guest cottage and herb garden and swimming pool. There's something pleasantly austere about Provençal gravel—it has a calm, cooling effect, setting off the wild and abundant vegetation and the hot sun. At the restaurant Chez Thomé, tables were placed on gravel in the shade of the trees. This casual country place is another family favorite, up there with the Four Dolphins. We walked across the gravel to our table as cicadas chirped in the nearby fields.

When my grandmother and great-aunt lived here in '59, they both rented houses a few miles from Aix; M.F.'s was along the Route du Tholonet, a winding road heading east out of town toward Le Tholonet, a small village in the shadow of Mont Ste.-Victoire. On the drive here, we'd tried in vain to spot the driveway to L'Harmas, the farmhouse she'd rented. It didn't matter—the road offered its own stunning dramas, curving through dry green hills and thickets of trees, Ste.-Victoire intimidating and stern in the distance. This is what's known as the Route Cézanne (he painted

these scenes in the 1890's), and it still looks that way, like a painting.

Coming into the center of town, we passed by the imposing Château du Tholonet, where M.F. had rented an apartment above the stables in the mid 50's, and my grandmother and her sons had visited. Describing her mealtime routines, M.F. wrote: "There was always that little rich decadent tin of 0lark pâté in the cupboard if I grew bored, or we could stroll down past the great ponds under the plane trees to the deft, friendly welcome of the Restaurant Thomé and eat a grilled pullet or a trout meunière, and an orange baked *a la norvegienne*.

As for us, we ordered beautiful green salads with red currants, a bit of foie gras, warm cheese with a red-pepper-and-garlic rémoulade, rabbit with a dried-fruit reduction, and *risotto aux fruits de mer*. I hesitate to write so hyperbolically, but I must say that it was a perfect lunch: perfect. Sitting under the trees in this unspeakably beautiful courtyard, at an informal table with my family and friends, I felt a connection to this place, and to Aix, that went beyond my own immediate experiences. I had come to find Aix, and found it was already in me, or to quote M.F. describing her arrival here all those years ago, "I was once more in my own place, an invader of what was already mine." ✚

resources

STAY

28 à Aix An intimate hotel in the city center. 28 Rue du 4 Septembre, Aix-en-Provence; 33-4/42-54-82-01; 28-a-aix. com; doubles from $$.

La Pauline A B&B on 20 acres of gardens. Les Pinchinats, 280 Chemin de la Fontaine des Tuiles, Aix-en-Provence; 33-4/42-17-02-60; lapauline. fr; doubles from $$.

HOUSE AND VILLA RENTALS

For longer stays and family groups, house rentals are an affordable option. **Here and Abroad** (610/228-4984; hereandabroad.com) owner Fabienne Perpiglia specializes in the Aix area, with some properties in other Provençal towns, and offers excellent, personalized service. **Hosted Villas** (800/374-6637; hostedvillas. com) and U.K.-based **Abercrombie & Kent Villas** (44-12/4254-7902; akvillas. com) both manage well-appointed rental properties.

EAT

Chez Thomé 74 Ave. Louis Destrem, Le Tholonet; 33-4/42-66-90-43; dinner for two ✗✗✗.

Les Deux Garçons 53 Cours Mirabeau, Aix-en-Provence; 33-4/42-26-00-51; dinner for two ✗✗.

L'Hostellerie de l'Abbaye de la Celle 10 Place du Général de Gaulle, La Celle; 33-4/98-05-14-14; dinner for two ✗✗✗✗.

SHOP

Aix Farmers' Market Place Richelme, Aix-en-Provence; 8 a.m. to 1 p.m. daily.

Aix Flower Market Place de l'Hôtel de Ville; Tues., Thurs., and Sat., 8 a.m. to 1 p.m.

Soulèo Provence Traditional French tableware. 2440 Chemin des Lauves, Aix-en-Provence; 33-4/42-93-04-54.

COOKING SCHOOL

Cooking with Friends in France Culinary-immersion programs. Plascassier; 562/221-1417; cookingwithfriends.com; five-day programs from ✗✗✗✗✗.

UNDISCOVERED GREECE

The province of Epirus, in northwestern Greece, is as pristine and uncrowded as it was 30 years ago, its rocky landscape just as dramatic. But new hotels are opening in areas like the Zagorohoria, where 44 traditional villages cling to the edge of the Vikos Gorge, said to be the world's deepest. Meanwhile, the once-sleepy capital, Ioánnina, has morphed into a fascinating city, its lakefront lined with lively cafés. Here are our favorite places to stay in the region.

Aristi Mountain Resort
This 18-room boutique hotel offers tasteful luxury in a mountain setting. Its restaurant, Salvia, serves gourmet versions of regional specialties, such as spinach *pites* (savory pies wrapped in homemade phyllo dough). Aristi; 30-265/304-1330; aristi.gr; doubles from $$.

Bourazani Wild Life Resort
On the Albanian border at the intersection of three rivers, this 20-room property is set in a 3,000-acre nature park filled with butterflies and wild orchids. Bourazani, Konitsa; 30-265/506-1283; bourazani. gr; doubles from $.

Grand Serai
An elegant hotel near the center of Ioánnina—and within walking distance of the lakeshore—the Grand Serai is a luxe interpretation of local Turkish-inspired architecture, with wooden balconies, lavish breakfasts, and Hermès amenities. 33 Dodonis, Ioánnina; 30-265/104-2884; mitsishotels.com; doubles from $$.

Hotel du Lac
On Ioánnina's lakefront, this 168-room property has live music around the pool on summer evenings. Akti Miaouli and Ikkou Sts., Ioánnina; 30-265/105-9100; hoteldulac.gr; doubles from $$.

Hotel Kastro
A simple but charming bed-and-breakfast located inside the city's historic walls—which are also home to two mosques turned museums, a synagogue, and a church. The hotel sits opposite an antiques store and below the Byzantine Museum. 57 Paleologou St., Ioánnina; 30-265/102-2866; ameliko.gr; doubles from $.

Lias Inn
The seven rooms have balconies overlooking a pavestone-covered square, scene of many a *panegyri*, the Greek holiday festival held every July. Lia; 30-266/404-1602; lias.gr; doubles from $.

Papaevangelou Guesthouse
Located near an entrance to the Vikos Gorge, the hotel is also close to a natural swimming hole off the road between Papingo and Mikro Papingo, two of the Zagorohoria's villages. Megalo Papingo; 30-265/304-1135; hotelpapaevangelou.gr; doubles from $.

Clockwise from above: Sunbathing along the Voïdomatis River, in Greece; a café on Ioánnina's lakefront; stone houses in the Zagorohoria; a plate of smoked meats at Salvia, Aristi Mountain Resort's restaurant; on a street in Ioánnina; a path among the stone structures at Aristi; the road between the villages of Aristi and Monodendri; *espresso freddo* at Salvia; a guest room at Aristi. Center: Outdoor dining in Ioánnina. Left: The ruins of the Kalogeriko bridge.

A satyr looking out from the garden at Villa Lante, in Bagnaia, Italy. Opposite: Hedges and stone pillars in the terraced garden at Villa Farnese, in Caprarola.

ROME'S GREEN EMPIRE

BY CHARLES MACLEAN
PHOTOGRAPHED BY CHRISTOPHER SIMON SYKES

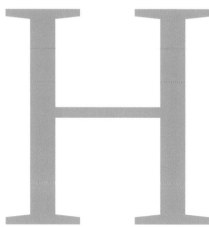

H IGH ABOVE THE SPANISH STEPS IN THE WOODED, statue-filled pleasure grounds of the Villa Medici, I find myself puffing heavenward up Pincio Hill, whose mini belvedere offers a 360-degree panorama of the Eternal City.

Lost in the astonishing view, I'm only half listening when our guide remarks that in the first century B.C. this same 17-acre site was covered by the Gardens of Lucullus. What she says next gets my full attention. The fabled gardens, created by a retired Roman general around his villa—somewhere under our feet—would become a model for other gardens in the city and later be recognized as one of the first attempts in the West to tame nature through landscape gardening.

This is where it all began. Right here.

In the company of friends who have come to look at villas and gardens in and around the city, I set off each day from the Hotel d'Inghilterra on sorties of enlightenment and varied delight. It's early May, the ideal time to be in Rome (fewer people; less traffic; the temperature in the balmy mid seventies) and to make excursions into its newly greened-up countryside. Fields of scarlet poppy and yellow mustard plants line the road to Bomarzo, a good hour north of the city by car and the first and most extraordinary of the gardens we visit.

Opposite: A fountain flanked by sculptures of river gods in repose, at Villa Lante.

More sculpture park than garden, Bomarzo's Sacro Bosco occupies a lush area on the grounds of the Villa Orsini. A web of looping trails leads though open glades, past rocky outcrops, and down steep ravines inhabited by giant, often grotesque statues of gods, mythical beasts, and other marvels. At every turn there's an encounter with some unexpected and eccentric work of art. An elephant with a tower on its back; a huge turtle bearing the statue of a goddess; a leaning stone fun house. Some of the moss-covered figures are badly worn and their symbolism long lost, but there's no mistaking the ogre whose gaping cave of a mouth (big enough to walk into without stooping) represents the entrance to the underworld.

If there's something melancholy about nature having reclaimed much of the "Parco dei Monstri," as it's known locally, it fits the spirit of the place and the story of its creator. In 1552, Prince Vicino Orsini started work on a Villa of Wonders for his beloved wife, who died tragically young, which caused the project to be shelved; it was later completed as a monument to her memory. On the morning of our visit, though, the woods are loud with birdsong and the sound of delighted laughter as groups of schoolchildren race around this Renaissance Disneyland, clambering over the monsters and being yelled at by exasperated teachers.

In *Italian Villas and Their Gardens* (1904), Edith Wharton points out that *villa* in Italian refers both to the house and its garden or pleasure grounds. At the Villa Lante, built for Cardinal Gambara in the 1560's on a hillside above the medieval town of Bagnaia and considered by many to be the finest Renaissance garden in Italy, the twin pavilions, or *palazzine*, play such a minor part in architect Giacomo Vignola's overall design they might as well be garden ornaments. In contrast to the fanciful exuberance of Bomarzo, only a few miles away, Villa Lante is all about order and proportion, if not restraint.

Its main terraces are subdivided by paths and box hedges into geometrical patterns; they're linked by steps and a central stream that falls from a grotto at the top of the garden through a sequence of magnificent fountains and cascades (adorned with shrimp tails, dolphins, and river gods) to the great water parterre that overhangs the ocher-roofed town below. As you look down on the garden from above, the beauty of these symmetrical arrangements becomes apparent—the sparkling play of sunlight on water; the inviting cool of ilex-shaded bowers—adding to the harmonious effect of the whole.

However remote from the modern concept of a garden—nothing much has changed since the French essayist Montaigne, strolling the paths here in 1581, admired the fountains for their beauty and grace and saw rainbow effects in the misty spray—you can still appreciate how Villa Lante achieves through its inspired design a bucolic sense of peace, which goes back to the classical ideal of balancing art and nature in country living.

After a simple yet delicious lunch at Il Borgo, a café-restaurant with tables on the main square in Bagnaia (the local mozzarella and house-made licorice-dark chocolate ice cream are memorable), we set off on a 20-minute

drive to the last garden of the day, in Caprarola. The only way to see what gardening authority Penelope Hobhouse called "one of the great masterpieces of Italian garden art" is by first taking the official tour of the Villa Farnese, a formidable pentagonal fortress that sits above the town looking out toward Rome. We troop through one magnificent empty salon after another (including a map-of-the-world room painted around 1570), and get a feel for how uncomfortable life must have been in those days, even for the rich and powerful.

It's a relief to emerge into the sunlit grounds behind the palace and wander uphill through mature woods of ilex, chestnut, and pine to the Casino del Piacere (House of Pleasure), a perfectly proportioned lodge also built by Vignola. The final approach to the casino is by way of a dramatic arrangement of steps and fountains leading to a terraced garden of stone pillars, 28 male and female busts on tall pedestals that seem to have sprung from the ground along with the sentinel cypresses. The grandeur may be a little daunting, but Caprarola illustrates the importance the late-Renaissance builders and their masters set on the relationship between villa, garden (with all its sculptural forms), and the surrounding landscape.

Above, from left: An ogre at Sacro Bosco, in Bomarzo; a gated passage within Rome's Botanical Garden.

THE NEXT MORNING, TAKING THE OLD APPIAN WAY out of Rome, we drive south for an hour toward Naples and stop, as travelers have been doing since Roman times, at Ninfa—a lush oasis in the desolate, once brigand-haunted Pontine Marshes. Here, tucked under the arid Lepini Hills, the ruins of a medieval town (razed by civil war in 1382) were gradually transformed over the course of the 20th century by the aristocratic, now died-out Caetani family into what some consider the most beautiful garden on earth.

There was never a formal plan. Three generations of Caetani wives helped Ninfa grow back over the skeleton of the abandoned town, its streets and buildings (tower, town hall, several churches) providing the framework for the garden. It still has a feeling of being inhabited not by ghosts but by the flora and fauna that have taken over the place, creating a dreamlike world of color, fragrance, and serenity.

A cypress avenue (once the main street) leads to grass paths (originally cobblestoned alleys) bordered with lavender and rosemary hedges that meander between the ruins. The crumbling stonework supports a profusion of climbing roses, clematis, honeysuckle, and jasmine. Vacant gateways and windows frame views of wildflower meadows, flowering shrubs, rare magnolias, pomegranate groves, and a cluster of giant timber bamboos. In the midday heat, the silence is broken only by the song of a nightingale and the water rushing from the crystal-clear stream that runs through Ninfa.

The sense of a natural equilibrium restored is as satisfying as it is humbling, but it's a reminder too of the vision and hard work that made and now preserve this heavenly spot.

One of its chief creators, Princess Marguerite Caetani, was American and a distant cousin of the poet T. S. Eliot. Besides importing and nurturing many exotic plant species, she founded the international literary magazine *Botteghe Oscure*, which flourished in the 1940's and 50's, and brought a succession of writers and artists to Ninfa. Her contributors make up a roll call of the giants—Lampedusa, Moravia, Calvino, Bertolt Brecht, Truman Capote, Carson McCullers, Tennessee Williams, Camus, and Malraux, to name a few. In my wanderings, I find the corner by the river where Giorgio Bassani wrote parts of *The Garden of the Finzi-Continis*, which he maintained was inspired by Ninfa and the Caetani family.

Leaving paradise, we drive up to the hilltop Caetani village of Sermoneta. Its great castle, once the seat of the Borgias, dominates the countryside. You can see clearly the oasis of Ninfa, an uneven patch of brilliant green among the browns and ochers of the surrounding fields, and the Pontine Marshes stretching to the hazy shores of the Mediterranean on one side and Rome on the other. ✢

resources

GARDENS

Botanical Garden
Established by Pope Nicholas III as a source of medicinal plants in the 13th century. 24 Largo Cristina di Svezia, Rome.

Garden of Orange Trees
Commemorates the Spanish orange tree planted here by Saint Dominic in the 13th century. Parco Savello, Piazza Pietro d'Illaria, Rome.

Gardens at Villa Aurelia
Centuries-old grounds bequeathed to the American Academy in 1911, with laurel hedges, tropical flora, and lemon trees. 1 Largo di Porta San Pancrazio, Rome; aarome.org; tours by appointment.

Gardens of Ninfa
68 Via Ninfina, Latina; 39-0773/632-231.

Janiculum Park
The gardens have city views and honor Giuseppe Garibaldi. Via Garibaldi, Janiculum Hill, Rome.

Rose Garden
A onetime cemetery for Rome's Jewish community; its central path is in the form of a menorah. Via di Valle Murcia, Rome.

Sacro Bosco
Villa Orsini, Bomarzo; 39-0761/924-029.

Villa Doria Pamphili
The park includes arches of an ancient aqueduct. Via di San Pancrazio, Rome.

Villa Farnese
Caprarola, near Viterbo; 39-0761/646-052.

Villa Lante
Via Jacopo Barozzi, Bagnaia; 39-0761/288-008.

Villa Medici
1 Viale Trinità dei Monti, Rome; 39-06/67611.

Villa Sciarra
Rare plants, plus sculptural decoration taken from several Lombard villas. Via Dandolo, Rome.

TOURS

Expert-led tours of Italy's gardens can be arranged by London-based **Fine Art Travel** (44-20/7437-8553; finearttravel.co.uk).

A fishing boat anchored along Gümüşlük Bay, on Turkey's Aegean shore.

by the sea

THE SWEET LIFE IN CAPRI

BY SIMON DOONAN
PHOTOGRAPHED BY JONATHAN SKOW

From left:
Jonathan Adler,
Simon Doonan,
and Trina Turk
sailing to the
Blue Grotto,
in Capri, Italy.
Opposite: A view
of the Faraglioni
rock formations,
near the
Marina Piccola.

Ah,

LA DOLCE VITA! FOR MOST PEOPLE, THIS INTOXICATING PHRASE IS SYNONYMOUS WITH ROME. Not for me. Reluctant though I am to irritate the ghost of Federico Fellini, I think the concept finds its fiercest and most fabulous expression on a certain little nugget in the Bay of Naples—Capri.

What makes the island so sweet? Just how *dolce* is the *vita*? How *dolce* are the *dolci*? How *dolce* is the Gabbana?

Capri is, first and foremost, a fatally appealing combination of rusticity and glamour. The juxtaposition of simple pleasures—plopping in the Med; hiking deserted cliffs; scarfing down bowls of fresh figs—with a full-throttle commitment to style makes for an extremely *dolce vita*. It also makes for great creative inspiration. As somebody who spends most of the year whirring like a hamster on the wheel of fashion, I naturally find it necessary to hop off and refuel every so often. Recently, I decided to seek relaxation and inspiration in Capri. My traveling companions are my designer/ceramicist husband, Jonathan Adler; L.A.-based fashion designer Trina Turk; and her photographer husband, Jonathan Skow. (On our trip, we avoid confusion by referring to the latter as Mr. Skow.) We spend a thoroughly *dolce* week at the legendary La Scalinatella. Eccentric and luxurious, "the Scally," as we affectionately dub it, looks as if it were decorated by Salvador Dalí after dropping acid. With its improbable collection of borderline-kitsch antiques and its stark white architecture, the Scally is the perfect base from which to sally forth and forage for inspiration.

JONATHAN IS ADDICTED TO BLUE: BABY BLUE, NAVY BLUE, AZURE BLUE—HE HAS YET TO MEET a blue that does not inspire a pot or a pillow for his stores. The blues of the water here—best viewed while swimming in a grotto—are incomparable. Trina is also something of a Med-head. She finds inspiration in every rock and ripple: the coral stripe that runs around the island and pops into view when the water is choppy suggests an entire beige-and-pink resort collection to her.

And then there's the people-watching. At La Fontelina—a bathing establishment that's great for a voyeuristic lunch—Trina takes further inspiration from the sighting of a bronzed Monica Vitti look-alike in a white cotton lace kurta with long flared sleeves over a teeny bikini. "White lace and a deep tan—a phenomenal combo," says Trina, as if writing the *Women's Wear Daily* review of her own upcoming show. Mr. Skow photographs the moment and, unsurprisingly, a white lace kurta appears in one of Trina's collections.

On every descent to the sea, Mr. Skow plays the role of intrepid paparazzo, hanging off cliffs and boat decks to get the perfect shot. He enjoys taking pictures without the usual ramparts of photo equipment, likening it to "swimming without a swimsuit—very liberating." One afternoon, Mr. Skow decides he wants an action shot of Jonathan and me diving off the side of our sailboat. Much to the amusement of Giancarlo, our captain, it takes about 15 tries before Mr. Skow finally gives the thumbs-up.

FROM THE KITSCHIEST ROCOCO TO THE COOLEST mod minimalism, our trip is a nonstop festival of Italian design. Every jaunt yields distracting visual stimuli. Whenever Jonathan walks through the lobby of our hotel, he gazes at the hallucinogenic blue-and-white floor tiles until he bumps into a fellow guest. And the futuristic, mod lounges that we encounter at the Giò Ponti–designed Hotel Parco dei Principi on a day trip to Sorrento are a personal favorite, as is the funky wall mural—made from shards of groovy Midcentury ceramic tchotchkes—at Gelateria Buonocore, a gelato shop across the street from Ferragamo back on Capri.

What really inspire us are the island's addictive boutiques. Trina can't get enough of the gaudy-but-chic handmade sandals. Jonathan feels a warm kinship with the uninhibited Caprese potters. Wandering around a souvenir shop near the docks, he snags a small abstract raku owl to send to his Peruvian workshop. He is determined to emulate the crackled glaze that garnishes the wings of the little creature.

And I find something else in the tiny stores of Capri—window-display inspiration. There is no space for the kind of dioramas that I install at Barneys. The Italians compensate for the absence of attention-getting props or rows of mannequins with something we fashion insiders call "merchandise handling." This technique reaches a zenith in the dinky window displays here: Malo cashmere sweaters are lusciously folded; Lacoste shirt collars are erect; D&G belts spill from crocodile shoes; perfectly pressed Hermès scarves ripple like the water that laps the side of Valentino's yacht down in the Marina Piccola. In the boutique displays, there is an innate finesse—the same finesse that the cook at Da Giorgio uses to arrange the shrimp and linguine on the plate with effortless panache—which inspires me because it points the spotlight back to what really matters: design and quality.

THE BEST PART OF ANY CAPRESE DAY IS THE MAGICAL passeggiata, the nocturnal stroll. Trina digs her nails into my arm as we watch this fashion spectacle one night: "For the last couple of years, women in the States have been wearing gray anti-fashion thrift-shop grunge," says Trina, as Mr. Skow snaps shots of long-legged beauties teetering down the cobblestones of the Via Camerelle in their Pucci party frocks and strappy gold Dolce & Gabbana sandals, "and this full-on commitment to adornment and glamour is what fashion is all about." "Transformation!" says Jonathan. "Exhibitionism!" I say.

Campy revelations aside, we all come away with something else, something pretty major, from our trip—a distinct feeling of optimism. Despite the lousy economy, the Capresi manage to keep an upbeat worldview. This is a reminder that *la dolce vita* is not a luxury destination, but a state of mind. Whether you are on a vacation, a stay-cation, or an inspira-cation, this *dolce* state of mind is yours for the taking. So put down your BlackBerry. What are you waiting for? ✚

Opposite: Shopping at a handmade-sandal store in Capri.

resources

STAY

Grand Hotel Quisisana 2 Via Camerelle; 800/745-8883 or 39-081/837-0788; quisisana. com; doubles from $$.

Hotel Gatto Bianco 32 Via Vittorio Emanuele; 39-081/ 837-0446; gattobianco-capri. com; doubles from $$.

Hotel Parco dei Principi 1 Via Bernardino Rota, Sorrento; 39-081/878-4644; doubles from $$.

J.K. Place Capri 225 Via Provinciale Marina Grande; 39-081/838-4001; jkcapri. com; doubles from $$$$.

La Scalinatella 8 Via Tragara; 39-081/837-0633; scalinatella.com; doubles from $$$.

Punta Tragara 57 Via Tragara; 39-081/837-0844; hoteltragara.com; doubles from $$$.

EAT

Da Giorgio 34 Via Roma; 39-081/837-5777; dinner for two ✘✘✘.

Da Luigi ai Faraglioni 5 Via Faraglioni; 39-081/837-0591; lunch for two ✘✘✘.

Faraglioni 75 Via Camerelle; 39-081/837-0320; dinner for two ✘✘✘.

Gelateria Buonocore 35 Via Vittorio Emanuele; 39-081/837-7826; gelato for two ✘.

Ristorante Aurora 18 Via Fuorlovado; 39-081/837-0181; dinner for two ✘✘✘.

Trattoria il Solitario 96 Via Giuseppe Orlandi; 39-081/ 837-1382; dinner for two ✘✘.

SHOP

Dsquared2 81 Via Camerelle; 39-081/838-8235.

Kiton 19 Piazzetta Umberto I; 39-081/838-8229.

Malo 6 Via Li Campi; 39-081/838-8254.

100% Capri 29 Via Fuorlovado; 39-081/837-7561.

Russo Uomo 8 Federico Serena; 39-081/838-8208.

ISLAND HIDEAWAYS

Endless sun, salty breezes, ocean for miles—and not a tourist in sight. There's nothing like venturing off the beaten path to discover an island that only the locals know about. Here, five places you can (almost) call your own.

Île d'Ouessant, France

Also known as "L'Île des Femmes" after the women who remained here while their fishermen husbands were at sea, this island in the English Channel is one of the Continent's most overlooked escapes. Rent a bike or hop a shuttle to the town of Lampaul, where you'll find crafts shops and crêpes, a specialty in Brittany. **Ti Jan Ar C'hafé** guesthouse *(33-2/98-48-82-64; hotels-de-charme-en-bretagne.com; doubles from $)*, half a mile inland, has eight spare rooms. Open the windows to hear the birds that nest nearby each spring. Tour Ouessant's five lighthouses before ferrying back to Brest or Le Conquet.

Favignana, Italy

On this butterfly-shaped isle near Sicily, the breeze is scented with jasmine and locals still catch bluefin tuna with nets and harpoons. Stay at the 46-room **Hotel Tempo di Mare** *(6 Via Frascia; 39-0923/922-474; hoteltempo dimare.it; doubles from $$)*, a tidy property with private balconies overlooking Levanzo, another small island. **Trattoria Due Colonne** *(76 Piazza Matrice, 39-0923/922-291; dinner for two ✕✕)* serves caponata, a Sicilian staple of eggplant, tomatoes, olives, and capers. Stock up on cured tuna *bresaola* at **La Casa del Tonno** *(12 Via Roma; 39-0923/*

922-227), then picnic at Cala Rossa, a secluded cove framed by white, craggy cliffs.

Alónnisos, Greece

The marine park on 14-mile-long Alónnisos, in the Northern Sporades, is home to the endangered Mediterranean monk seal. The island is awash with color—ruby-red flowers, pale yellow cliffs, and green olive groves amid ancient villages, pebble beaches, and walking trails to explore. See some of the more than 25 churches, many dating back to the 16th century, with **Alónnisos Walks** *(alonnisoswalks.co.uk)*. Five minutes by car from the harbor, the **Atrium of Alónissos Hotel** *(30-242/406-5750; atriumalonnissos.gr; doubles from $)* has 29 rooms updated with mosaic tiling and cheery curtains, chairs, and bedspreads.

Oaxen, Sweden

The picturesque spot south of Stockholm (imagine bright cottages planted among stands of birch and elm) is fast becoming a culinary destination. At the minimalist **Oaxen Krog** *(46-855/153-105; four-course prix fixe dinner for two ✕✕✕✕✕)*, chef Magnus Ek prepares regionally sourced dishes such as birch-smoked salmon and grilled Skilleby cucumber. After dinner, you can retire to the *Prince van Orangiën (46-855/153-105;*

princen.se; doubles from $$), the restaurant's seven-cabin 1930's Dutch riverboat-hotel docked steps away. In nearby Södertälje, visit **Tullgarn Palace** *(46-855/572-011; royalcourt.se)*, famous for its Rococo interiors and English gardens.

Bozcaada, Turkey

With its Ottoman-Greek whitewashed houses and lack of tourism, Bozcaada, one of Turkey's two Aegean islands, has unspoiled vistas at every turn, plus a 2,000-year-old wine-making tradition. At **Corvus Vineyards** *(90-286/697-8181; corvus.com.tr)*, Reşit Soley produces the country's most sought-after bottles. Stay at **Kaikias Hotel** *(Kale Arkasi Mevkii; 90-286/697-0250; kaikias.com; doubles from $)*, with 22 rustic-chic rooms in the shadow of a Byzantine fortress. Don't miss the red mullet and smoked octopus at the 110-year-old **Lodos** *(Çinar Çari Cad., 90-286/697-0545; dinner for two ✕✕)*, and bring home a jar of house-made poppy jam, sold at **Ada Café** *(4 Çinar Çeşme Sk.; 90-286/697-8795)*, near the main square.

Clockwise from above: Votsi Bay, off Alónnisos, Greece; a bluff on France's Île d'Ouessant; *Prince van Orangiën*'s Captain's Cabin, in Oaxen, Sweden; a street in Favignana, Italy; the port of Bouguesen, on Île d'Ouessant; *Prince van Orangiën*'s Chief Mate's Cabin; sheep on the Turkish island of Bozcaada; a guest room at Favignana's Hotel Tempo di Mare; olives for sale at La Casa del Tonno, also in Favignana. Center: A quiet alleyway on Favignana.

THE BALTIC RIVIERA

BY THOMAS BELLER
PHOTOGRAPHED BY BLASIUS ERLINGER

It ALL STARTED DURING A LONG CONSULTATION WITH A map. I was staring at the French Riviera, where we were thinking of spending a week. At some point my eye drifted upward until I hit a patch of blue, the Baltic Sea, and the filigreed curtain of Danish islands that separates it from the Atlantic. The looming fingers of the Scandinavian countries extended down from above, and the sea came to a timorous stop at the western tip of Russia. At its bottom lip were Latvia and Estonia. Looking at the map I couldn't help thinking of them as two tiny pebbles only recently revealed by the receding Soviet tide. They have been independent since 1991 and joined the European Union in 2003. But at the moment, my thoughts were less geopolitical than preoccupied with the hedonistic question, *What's the beach like up there?* Mustn't there be a Baltic Riviera? Surely it must be pristine, untouched, an unknown kingdom neglected by history (or the tourism industry).

Which is how I found myself, a few months later, with my wife and our six-month-old daughter (a.k.a. "the Nugget"), setting off from Riga International Airport for Jūrmala, Latvia, the best-known beach resort on the Baltic. I'd had this perverse idea that we'd be entering some sort of Soviet time machine, but when I saw the profusion of Mercedes, BMW, and Audi sedans surrounding us on the highway, I knew I'd been wrong. What I discovered were two Baltic countries, different in language and culture, that are struggling to define themselves against their enormous neighbor to the east.

JŪRMALA IS MADE UP OF A SERIES OF BEACHES STRETCHED OUT OVER A SMALL PENINSULA, bordered by the Lielupe River on one side and the Baltic on the other. The main promenade, Jomas Iela, sits next to Majori, the most popular beach, and is surrounded by thick trees, beneath which is an interesting amalgam of 19th-century wooden villas built for vacationing Russians—some are very beautiful, with towers, spires, and elaborate porches—alongside new structures with minimalist Scandinavian architecture. All the buildings—a jumble of old-school and new—were built in scale to the surrounding forest, except for two. One is the Jūrmala Spa Hotel, where we were staying: 11 stories of purple-tinted glass rising up out of the woods. Inside, the lobby hummed with a techno beat, and on the walls were black-and-white "art photographs" that celebrated the nude female body. I held my daughter tight and wondered what I had gotten us into.

Opposite: Jumping into the Baltic Sea from a dock at Pädaste Manor, on the Estonian island of Muhu.

A glass elevator lifted us up over the trees and took my mood with it. I was pleased when we opened the door to our small but opulent room on the 11th floor and saw that, in addition to the sea, the beach, the forest, and the river, our view encompassed the white wedding cake of the Baltic Beach Hotel, the other enormous building on the beach that had been my first choice (and fully booked).

The Nugget had a boo-boo, and so we set off on the promenade to find a Band-Aid. There I discovered that Jūrmala, long favored among Russians, is not yet a place where English is widely spoken. But pantomiming "Band-Aid?" with a baby in your arms is not difficult. This errand taken care of, we walked to the beach for our Baltic baptism. Majori was impressively huge—a stretch of soft white sand that runs in either direction as far as you can see. And it was absolutely packed. But there was something odd about it: the dividing line between beach and water was not clear. Instead, people were sitting and lounging in the water 30 feet out from where it lapped the shore.

We waded in, trailing the Nugget's toes in the surprisingly warm water. I had expected that, even in August, it would be freezing. But the Baltic is shallow, so the sun warms it, and there are hardly any waves. We walked 50 yards out to sea. Ahead of us, a group of teenagers screamed as the water swelled to their waists.

That night, at one of the outdoor restaurants that line Jomas Iela, we sat among the beachgoers and families from Riga who come for dinner on weekends. Amid the gingerbread architecture, you can also buy ice cream and cotton candy, sit in a rowdy beer garden, or take a small-scale amusement park ride. A good portion of the citizenry dresses up for the night, in a mix of backless halter tops and elegant evening wear, and this promenading enhances the faintly czarist atmosphere.

Later we returned to our room and saw the Baltic Beach Hotel lit up like a cruise ship surrounded by darkness. It was graced with a huge neon sign with some malfunctioning letters. And so we drifted pleasantly off to sleep that first night with the words BALTIC BEACH HO looming over the town, the forest, and the sea.

AFTER TWO NIGHTS IN JŪRMALA WE HEADED WEST toward the port town of Ventspils to begin our trip to Muhu, a small Estonian island to the north. Beneath the bright blue sky were fields dotted with round bales of hay, sloping gently toward the horizon. We passed thick stands of white birches and dense forest with an incongruously sandy floor that suggested the nearness of the sea. Now and then we'd see a picturesque house sitting alone by the side of the road. The landscape began to take on the flavor of one of the quaint—but also dark and foreboding—tales of the Brothers Grimm.

At the outskirts of Ventspils, gray Soviet-era housing blocks rose from the fields. One of them, an unfinished skeleton, looked almost archaeological, a ruin from the previous empire. We drove past little houses, each with a fastidiously tended garden out front. They made the town seem house-proud and tidy. Ventspils is an ice-free port where Russian oil and minerals are loaded onto ships. It is bisected by the Venta River, over which rises an elevated bridge that swept us up and then gently deposited us in the center of the sleepy old port town. Our room that night, in the Hotel Vilnis, was modest and clean. Only the convention of attack-dog trainers, whose dogs were barking in cages outside the lobby, made the visit the slightest bit unsettling.

The next morning we woke very early and drove to the ferry to cross over to the neighboring island of Saaremaa. As we set off, I noticed a line of tankers running parallel to our course, sailing along the horizon in a way that made the world seem flat. A vague fantasy of the naval maneuvers on the Baltic—both those of the 15th century, when the Swedes fought the Russians for control of the region, and those of the 20th century, when the Germans battled the Soviets—emanated from that line of ships and stayed with me until we landed on Saaremaa. Under Soviet rule, it and Muhu were part of the "border zone." No one—not even Estonians—could travel to the area without a visa, and even since becoming part of the European Union, the islands have seen few visitors and little in the way of economic development.

Once on Muhu's southern shore, we located Pädaste Manor, a series of low stone houses and a main house arranged around a beautiful quad. Thick old trees sway high above the lawn, which is intersected by paths that lead to a gate and a long, thin strait of water to the Baltic. We dropped off our bags at our attractive duplex room and rushed to the Sea House restaurant to eat. It was nearly three in the afternoon, and we had the place to ourselves. The stone walls felt so heavy and protective that each small window seemed like its own miniature Dutch Renaissance painting, capturing landscapes of

iridescent green grass, pale light, and calm if slightly ominous water in the distance.

I wanted to get into the carnivorous, hunter-gatherer vibe of the place as much as possible, and, not being able to decide between the roasted and dried ostrich and the moose carpaccio, I chose the "Muhu antipasti," which had them both, along with smoked eel and something called "dried roach." (The roach, I was relieved to discover, is a small fish found in the rivers and creeks of western Estonia.) The moose carpaccio was fantastic, like pork but smokier and gamier. Elizabeth had the squab. Sated, I left her and the Nugget in the room for a nap and headed out past the gate. There, amid the tall grass, I found a helipad and, beyond that, a dock at the foot of the long lane of water stretching out to the sea. The sun was setting now, though the sky had a couple of hours of daylight left in it. I lay down on the pier and looked up at the sky, and then sat up to take in the stillness of it all, the distant shore dark with trees, the streaks of pink light playing on the water.

The next morning I met Martin Breuer, the Dutch-born proprietor of the manor, who told me about the island's history. Muhu has only been accessible since 1992. "There was never any Sovietization, no shipping in workers from Russia, and so tradition and culture survived much better here than in other parts of Estonia," he said. Built by German aristocrats in the 19th century, Pädaste, he explained, was one of the few manor houses in Estonia that had not been built over by the state during the Soviet era. "Most of them now have corn silos, or ugly apartment blocks."

Breuer came to look at the place in 1993 and, after purchasing it three years later, has rarely left. Estonia then had a kind of innocence, he said. "In '93 you'd come to a bar, there were three bottles of hard liquor and four bartenders. And everyone sat together and sang songs. Now there is so much energy. You feel a people building their country."

On the last morning there, I had my hay treatment. The Baltic States have retained the old-world idea that holidays should be more than just fun: they should be restorative, curative—as though the Baltic itself were a kind of aquatic version of the Magic Mountain. For a moment, the line separating the height of luxury and medieval punishment seemed very thin. I was wrapped in a giant gauzy tea bag packed with hay and told by the young woman attending to me to lie down on a plank

Opposite, from left: Medieval rooftops in the Old Town of Tallinn, Estonia; cruising the city's cobblestoned streets aboard a Segway.

suspended over a wooden vat of warm water. With the press of a button, the plank beneath me miraculously folded itself into a kind of easy chair and I was lowered into the vat and left to steep.

The rich, grassy aroma of the hay began to percolate into my nostrils. The whole thing combined a kind of return to the womb and a return to the manger—thus appealing to fantasies both Freudian and biblical, along with the as-yet-uncategorized desire to be wrapped in a tea bag and dunked in hot water. When it was over I was led to a goat-milk massage by a young woman with platinum hair and multiple piercings.

I didn't want to break the mood too much, but I couldn't help asking, "Is this special hay?"

"No," she replied. "It's just hay."

"The brochure implies there is some special property in Estonian hay."

"Well, the hay is from Estonia," she said. "But I'm not sure what the special properties might be."

"How do you get it?"

"We mow the lawn."

I WOUND MY WAY OUT OF TALLINN'S OLD TOWN at dusk. I was going east, to the city of Narva on the Russian border, where, I had been told, I would find the Baltic's most spectacular beach. That morning Elizabeth, the Nugget, and I had made our way to the capital—a pleasant ferry ride followed by two hours on a highway into Estonia's capital. There, I had set up Elizabeth and the Nugget in the newly opened Hotel Telegraaf, which occupies the renovated interior of the former post office at the center of the Old Town. With its black marble and glittering chandeliers, it exuded a solidity that made me comfortable leaving the two of them in their room.

I had been led to believe that Narva was Estonia's equivalent to the South Bronx, so I was doing this part of the journey on my own. I guided the car through the narrow cobblestoned streets of the Old Town, where the buildings seemed huddled together and medieval but also strikingly colorful and clean. In their brightness I felt the pulsating prosperity of the place.

I took a winding road to a beautiful little beach populated only by some youths setting up a campfire and a volleyball net. I looked at the waves, tempted, but there was no time for a swim. I had to get to Narva to meet a local journalist who had agreed to show me around. A few miles outside of town I started passing trucks parked on the side of the road, one after another—a petrified forest of them. The Russian border is just across the river ahead. For the truck drivers, crossing it here can take more than a week. Estonia may have modernized—Tallinn is now home to Skype, the Internet phone company—but as my guide, journalist Sergei Stepanov, himself a Russian, later explained, "On the Russian side they are all drunk!"

---

resources

STAY

Baltic Beach Hotel 23/25 Juras St., Majori, Jūrmala, Latvia; 371-67/771-400; balticbeach.lv; doubles from $$.

Hotel Jūrmala Spa 47/49 Jomas St., Jūrmala, Latvia; 371-67/784-400; hoteljurmala.lv; doubles from $$.

Hotel Telegraaf 9 Vene St., Tallinn, Estonia; 372/600-0600; telegraafhotel.com; doubles from $.

Hotel Vilnis 5 Talsu, Ventspils, Latvia; hotelvilnis.lv; 371-63/668-800; doubles from $.

Pädaste Manor Muhu, Estonia; 372/454-8800; padaste.ee; doubles from $$.

EAT

Melnais Sivens Small tavern that serves hearty stews and local seafood, in a medieval castle. 17 Jana, Ventspils, Latvia; 371-63/622-396; dinner for two XX.

Sea House Pädaste Manor, Muhu, Estonia; 372/454-8800; dinner for two XX.

Veski Tavern Estonian food and live music in a 100-year-old windmill. 19 Parna Tn., Kuressaare, Estonia; 372/453-3776; dinner for two X.

DO

Estonian Song and Dance Celebration Festival 95 Narva Nantee, Tallinn, Estonia; laulupidu.ee; July.

Kumu Art Museum Estonian paintings and sculpture from before and after the Soviet era. 34 Weizenbergi, Valge 1, Tallinn, Estonia; 372/602-6001; ekm.ee.

Latvian National Opera Opera and ballet season runs September–May, with a festival in June highlighting new works. 3 Aspazijas Bulvaris, Riga, Latvia; 371-67/073-777; opera.lv.

We met at a petrol station at the edge of town, and he drove me to the beach I had heard about. Some State Department guys in Tallinn had told me this was the secret gem of the Baltic—better than Jūrmala. Perhaps it was my source, or the proximity of the Russian border, but I felt a bit like a spy. We drove past a huge monument featuring a tank sitting on top of a square pedestal with fresh flowers arranged at its base, down a quiet lane, then pulled up to a small carriage painted in red-and-white candy stripes and sitting at the edge of a little park.

Stepanov got out and proudly announced that this was the symbol of the town. "A cabin for the shy girls who wanted to go to the beach in the beginning of the last century," he said. Apparently these "shy girls" would enter the carriage fully clothed and change into their bathing gear, after which it would be pulled, either by horses or men, into the shallows. I couldn't decide what was more touching—the image of the beach dotted with these carriages, with ladies emerging and returning, or the cheerful hope and optimism embodied by the fresh coat of paint on this specimen and the nearby plaque explaining its history.

We walked down the beach. It was mostly empty. Stepanov pointed out a yellow gazebo. "Tchaikovsky used to compose there," he said. Now it was covered with crudely drawn graffiti—anti-American and anti-Estonian slogans, written by the angry Russian youth of Narva. Narva had once been the Hamptons of St. Petersburg, 85 miles away. The dirt road behind the beach was lined with gorgeous old wooden mansions, some in disrepair. The center of things had shifted to Jūrmala. When I asked why, Stepanov said, "Politics." The fundamental tension of Estonia lies in its desire to separate entirely from its old Soviet occupiers. And yet a third of the population is Russian and doesn't even speak Estonian. Many of these immigrants live in Narva. Could Narva rise again? There is no way to know. But that broad expanse of empty beach seemed promising.

On my drive back to Tallinn, clouds raced across a bright blue sky, and I raced along with them, heading toward my wife and the Nugget. I passed more houses with steeply angled roofs and meadows dotted with haystacks. I drove across a huge field of wind turbines—their narrow bases and three blades so gigantic it was surreal, like toys in a race of giants. The windmills were spinning to the rhythm of the clouds racing overhead, the future in the landscape of a fairy tale. ✚

THE NEW CLASSICS

Europe's quintessential resort areas (St.-Tropez, Capri, Santorini) continue to draw jet-setters in droves. But now the scene—and the glitzy hotels and restaurants that dominate it—is expanding to less expected shores. Here, three new escapes with rising cachet.

The New St.-Tropez

Cornwall, England
A sun-starved crowd heads to Britain's southwestern coast for its golden sands and ambitious restaurants. Stay at the **Scarlet Hotel** *(Tredragon Rd., Mawgan Porth; 44-1637/861-800; scarlethotel. co.uk; doubles from $$)*, an eco-lodge and spa where all 37 rooms have access to cliff-edge hot tubs and Atlantic Ocean views. For local steamed mussels, dine at BBC chef Rick Stein's **Cornish Arms** pub *(Churchtown, St. Merryn, Padstow; 44-1841/ 520-288; dinner for two XX)*.

The New Capri

Valletta, Malta
Situated on a small island in the Mediterranean, this UNESCO World Heritage site is attracting globe-trotters with updated hotels, cafés, and wine bars. **Maison La Vallette** *(St. Patrick's St.; 356/7948-8047; vallettasuites. com; doubles from $)* has limestone walls and Alessi furnishings, while **Caffé Cordina** *(244/5 Republic St.; 356/2123-4385; lunch for two XX)*, one of Malta's oldest coffee shops, serves sweet treats such as honey rings made with black treacle syrup.

The New Santorini

Korčula, Croatia
This region is known for its wild Adriatic scenery, Venetian Renaissance architecture, and small-scale vineyards. Travelers are flocking to the hotel of choice: **Lešić Dimitri Palace** *(1-6 Don Pavla Poše; 385-20/715-560; lesic-dimitri. com; doubles from $$)*, housed in a historic bishop's palace, with five individually designed suites. At the property's bar, LD, on a terrace overlooking the Mediterranean, sample Croatia's renowned wines, including the citrusy Grk.

CORNWALL, ENGLAND

KORČULA, CROATIA

VALLETTA, MALTA

Clockwise from right: Boats moored off Korčula Island, in Croatia; a stretch of the Dalmatian coast; the pool at the Scarlet Hotel, in Cornwall, England; a sampling of Cornwall's *fruits de mer*; a traditional house in the county; St. Ursula Street in Valletta, Malta; a view of Valletta's Grand Harbor; a guest room at Maison La Vallette; a nun near Korčula's Cathedral of St. Mark. Center: Cornwall's pristine shoreline.

Sailboats in the harbor at Maçakizi resort, in Türkbükü, Turkey. Opposite: A waiter at the hotel's beach club.

ALONG THE TURKISH COAST

BY PETER JON LINDBERG
PHOTOGRAPHED BY CEDRIC ANGELES

I

MEAN, IF YOU'RE GOING TO LOUNGE AROUND ON THROW PILLOWS AT A
beach club, sipping chilled raki or rosé while being serenaded by seabirds and
Cesária Évora, there's arguably no finer place to do it. And if, like any normal
person, your holiday agenda is to sit still—lifting your head now and then to
admire a passing sailboat, or the genetic spectacle of some raven-haired Central
European heiress—you could hardly do better than the Bodrum Peninsula, a
swath of rock, sand, cypress, and cedar that reaches from Turkey's southwest coast into the stained-
glass blue of the Aegean. ("Bodrum" refers to the largest town and to the peninsula as a whole.) Though
the region has a wealth of historical and architectural heritage, the majority of its visitors—2.9
million of them a year, mostly Turks, Brits, and other Europeans—come to relax on the beach, to
relax somewhere near the beach, or to relax at cliff-top resorts with stunning views of the beach.

They do not, in other words, come to spend their waking hours sweltering in a rented 4 x 4,
driving every last dusty road in search of something more interesting than a beach. I, however, have a
problem sitting still. Cursed with restless legs, I can never simply enjoy where I am, even if where I am
is a splendid Aegean summer resort. (This drives my wife, Nilou, a little crazy, but she indulges me.)
Europeans might be jaded by ancient ruins, Crusades-era castles, and centuries-old fishing villages,
but we didn't fly all this way to lie on a beach. Let others laze around sipping rosé: I wanted to see the
real Bodrum. From the moment Nilou and I checked into our hotel—Maçakizi, in the north-coast
town of Türkbükü, 30 minutes from Bodrum—I was ready to turn around and hit the road.

ON A PENINSULA WITH ITS SHARE OF OPULENT VILLAS AND OVER-THE-TOP RESORTS, MAÇAKIZI
(pronounced mah-cha-*kiz*-uh) is a standout, the sexiest hotel in all of Bodrum. That it's hardly a
traditional hotel is one reason: it feels more like the shoreside estate of some globe-trotting Turkish
family blessed with considerable wealth but also the good sense to keep things simple. The property
unfolds along a hillside studded with olive trees, tangerine groves, and bursts of bougainvillea. Eighty-
one guest rooms are minimally but tastefully furnished and swathed in creamy white, punctuated
by the bold abstract canvases of Turkish painter Suat Akdemir. Balconies offer knockout views of
the harbor.

In July and August that harbor fills up with yachts and impossibly tall sailing ships, their masts
piercing the sky like minarets. Launches glide to and fro across the water, delivering their owners

Opposite: A view of the
Castle of St. Peter, a
15th-century fortress
on Bodrum's harbor.

to shore. Many of them alight at Maçakizi, whose beach club is a landmark in Türkbükü: a series of wooden decks over the water, strewn with white cushions and pillows, shaded by sailcloth canopies and twig-roofed pavilions. The water is clear and generally calm, sheltered within a semiprivate cove. Every so often the muezzin's call to prayer drifts across the water from the town mosque, a trebly counterpoint to the languid jazz playing at the bar.

Maçakizi is, in fact, owned by a globe-trotting Turkish family. Ayla Emiroglu, who moved here from Istanbul in 1977, runs the hotel with her son, Sahir Erozan, a former restaurateur who spent two decades in the power-dining rooms of Washington, D.C. At Maçakizi, the guest list alone is intriguing: Caroline Kennedy, Chelsea Clinton, Antonin Scalia, and Ruth Bader Ginsburg have all vacationed here, along with the requisite Turkish music and film stars. During the summer, paparazzi float in Zodiacs just offshore, training telephoto lenses on Maçakizi's decks.

While it's definitely a scene in high season, Erozan does his best to keep the atmosphere refined, the crowd just this side of raucous. And the food—served on a breezy terrace just above the beach—is fabulous, particularly the lunch buffet, with its tantalizing array of Turkish kebabs and meze: flaky spinach *börek*, stuffed peppers spiked with cloves, and a smoky *patlican salatasi* (eggplant purée) that haunts me still.

BUT I COULDN'T LEAVE WELL ENOUGH ALONE. AFTER a single day at the resort, I was anxious to explore. And so each morning, my wife and I set out in the 4 x 4, armed with a stack of guidebooks and three useless maps. (More on those later.) We were, I think, the only guests who'd rented a car; most had arrived by boat, taxi, or limousine. We were definitely the only guests who took our car back *out* each day, after a hasty sunrise breakfast. The valets didn't know what to make of us. "You want to go *where*?" Or, as one guest put it: "Why?" Everyone at Maçakizi seemed happy right where they were.

Too bad for them, for there's plenty to see around the peninsula. The crumbling windmills and stone churches left by Greek Orthodox settlers. The white-domed *gümbets*, or cisterns, that dot the parched terrain (and inspire the look of so many villa developments). The rustic villages, tumbling down steep hillsides to the sea, with their beguiling, inscrutable names—Gündoğan!

Akyarlar! Yalikavak! Not least, the Old Town of Bodrum itself, with its trellised pedestrian lanes and its 15th-century Castle of St. Peter towering over the harbor.

Though Europeans tend to treat the Bodrum Peninsula like an Aegean St.-Tropez, in the more rugged corners it better recalls Croatia's Dalmatian Coast: both share that moody, haunting beauty that attends any place where the long-dead outnumber the living. There were quotidian finds as well, mostly of the edible sort. On a commercial strip outside Bodrum town we stumbled upon a *kebapci* (kebab house) called Denizhan, and our favorite meal of the trip: skewers of spicy grilled lamb, brick-oven *pide* (Turkey's improvement on pizza), and ethereal house-baked lavash bread. And at Bodrum's Friday produce market, we were the only travelers in sight, ogling sunset-hued zucchini blossoms, musk-scented melons, and peaches plucked that morning, still dewy from the orchard.

What I hadn't accounted for was the heat. We'd arrived in the vicious heart of July. That week the thermometer hit 104 degrees. Men slumped, like zombies, in café chairs, scarcely able to hoist their frappés. Dogs cowered in doorways, glassy-eyed and whimpering. In the sunblasted courtyards of St. Peter's Castle, we watched one of the resident peacocks trot up to a Swedish tourist and fan its spectacular plumage, in a vain attempt to cool itself. The Swede just stared blankly at the bird, too hot to bother snapping a photo.

And then there were the maps. At an Istanbul bookshop I'd purchased three Bodrum road maps, so intent was I on missing nothing. By the end of our trip I had torn the first and second to bits and crumpled the third into a tiny, unrecognizable ball. In hindsight, I see my rage was misplaced. It had been my impression that the maps were crudely drawn and poorly labeled. I now realize that *Bodrum* was crudely drawn and poorly labeled. Street names are nonexistent, road signs a rarity. Endless switchbacks defy spatial logic. Thankfully, locals are willing to help. Driving in from the airport, we stopped to ask three men if they could point the way to Maçakizi. After some confusing back-and-forth, one jumped into his car and led us the remaining six miles to the hotel. "Hard to explain," he said sheepishly, then waved good-bye.

So the heat and the maps put a damper on our explorations. By 3 p.m. we'd turn back, exhausted, to Maçakizi, change into our swimsuits, and hit the decks.

Here, people had more sense. None of *them* had broken a sweat. For the beautiful Maçakizians, sightseeing was limited to ogling their own cartoonish bodies: an all-day parade of gazelle-like women and the men who love them, or at least pay for their drinks. The women change bikinis after every dip in the water—seven, eight times in an afternoon, each swimsuit with a corresponding (and wholly ineffective) cover-up.

Suffice it to say, I have trouble picturing Justice Ginsburg here. What does she wear? A black terry-cloth robe? Watching the gazelles and their consorts, we felt both over- and underdressed: overdressed in that *our* swimsuits had more surface area than a cocktail napkin; underdressed in that they weren't encrusted with rhinestones. What a difference a few decades makes.

IN THE 1960'S, THE TOWN OF BODRUM WAS A backwater of 5,100. The summer population now tops half a million. Erozan recalls a quieter time. When his mother arrived in 1977, "Bodrum was like a little Positano, or Key West in Hemingway's day—full of bohemians, writers, painters," he says. "You'd sit at a café and see Rudolf Nureyev; at the other table, Mick Jagger."

In the shadow of Bodrum's castle, Ayla Emiroglu opened a modest bed-and-breakfast, and called it Maçakizi—after her own nickname, Turkish for queen of spades. Over the years she upgraded and expanded the place, eventually relocating it to the north coast. "There were no roads in Türkbükü at the time," Erozan says. "If you wanted to build, you carried everything in from the sea." In 2000, Maçakizi moved across the bay to its current site. Emiroglu still lives above the resort, in a house with views of the once-sleepy bay that she, as much as anyone, helped put on the global map.

Erozan admits to misgivings about Bodrum's explosion of development. Hillsides are filling up with extravagant villa complexes (including one designed by Richard Meier), while formerly isolated coves are colonized by international resorts. "Sometimes I think we grow too much in this country," Erozan says. "In Italy, the old things stay in place, like in a painting. But here we build so much that we're losing the charm of what Bodrum was."

Bodrum today is really two places, depending on when you visit. July and August bring the Arabian princes, Scandinavian swimwear models, and assorted Eurotrash scenesters. Better to come in late spring or

Above, from left: House-made *pide* at Maçakizi's restaurant; the resort's beach-bar scene.

Sahir Erozan, co-owner of Maçakizi. This page, clockwise from right: Doğal Dondurma, an ice cream stand in Türkbükü; accessories at a local boutique; the Limon Café, in Gümüşlük.

Rabbit Island,
as seen
from across
Gümüşlük bay.
This page,
clockwise from
left: Dancing
on Bar Street;
the morning
catch off the
dock at Mimoza,
a restaurant in
Gümüşlük; a
guest emerging
from Türkbükü
Bay at Maçakizi.

early fall, when the peninsula returns—somewhat—to its quieter, less pretentious self.

Or you could go at any time of year to Gümüşlük (pronounced ga-*moosh*-luk), on the peninsula's western coast. Since the seventies, the village has drawn a hippie/lefty contingent; in the shops along the main drag, women with henna-dyed hair sell scented oils and evil-eye bracelets. The beach is lined with fish restaurants, from boisterous family joints to romantic, votive-lit spots with tables in the sand. Try Mimoza, where the grilled octopus and calamari are sensational. A few hundred yards offshore is Tavsan Adan, a.k.a. Rabbit Island, which you can wade to at low tide to hike among the resident colony of wild bunnies. When the sun is high and the water clear, you can glimpse the remains of ancient Myndos—the Hellenic village that now lies submerged in the lagoon, yards below the surface.

Speaking of things hiding in plain sight, I'm ashamed to say that it took us six days of driving all over the Bodrum Peninsula before we discovered that our favorite place was right next door: the pedestrian promenade that fronts Türkbükü Harbor, starting just south of Maçakizi. Why we didn't venture here earlier is a source of great embarrassment. (From our cove it was obscured by a hill.) It turned out we could walk there in two minutes. The promenade traces a half-moon along the shore, winding around (and occasionally through) the many waterside restaurants, guesthouses, boutiques, and nightclubs. The northern section, closer to Maçakizi, is trendier, louder, and more international; farther south, the crowd and vibe grow more local. Here, Turkish music—not Kanye—plays in the bars. Families stroll the waterfront until late in the evening, stopping at snack carts for roasted mussels, grilled corn, and cups of tart, fresh-pressed mulberry juice.

And if you *really* want your mind blown, you'll follow the path until you come upon the perpetual line outside Doğal Dondurma. I'm going to go out on a limb here and call this THE BEST ICE CREAM IN ALL OF TURKEY, because I simply can't conceive of anything better. Doğal's ever-shifting flavors include *kavun* (honeydew), *visne* (sour cherry), *seftali* (peach), and, best of all, *mandalina*, a sorbet made from tart Bodrum tangerines.

Once we found it, a walk along the harbor became our twice-daily routine—always ending at Doğal Dondurma to try some exotic new flavor, usually consumed on a pier with our feet dangling in the water. Afternoons on the promenade proved far preferable to sweating in the 4 x 4, which we now happily left to bake in the hotel parking lot. There was surely more to see, but here in Türkbükü we had all we needed: the sun warming our backs, the Aegean cooling our toes, and untold flavors of ice cream to taste. ✚

resources

STAY

4 Reasons Hotel & Bistro
Simple but chic 20-room hotel set amid olive groves outside the charming village of Yalikavak. 2 Bakan Cad., Yalikavak; 90-252/ 385-3212; 4reasonshotel. com; doubles from $.

Maçakizi Kesire Mevkii, Türkbükü; 90 252/377 6272; macakizi.com; doubles from $$; closed October–April.

EAT

Çimentepe Boisterous seafood palace that comes alive after dark. Order the grilled octopus (*izgara ahtapot*) and excellent zucchini-flower dolma (*kabak cicegi dolmasi*). Gerisalti Mevkii, Yalikavak; 90-252/385-4237; dinner for two XXX.

Denizhan Unassuming highway-side *kebapci* with a delightful terrace out back. The kebabs and *lahmajun pide* are both stellar. Muğla Bodrum Yolu, Konacik;

90-252/353-7675; lunch for two XX.

Doğal Dondurma
Promenade, Türkbükü; 90-252/363-9345; ice cream for two XX.

Limon Café Convivial bar/café beloved for its sunset views and cocktails. 1 Yali Mevkii, Gümüşlük; 90-252/394-4044; drinks for two XX.

Mimoza Booked up nightly by a sophisticated crowd. The fish is generally fantastic, and priced accordingly. Yali Mevkii; Gümüşlük; 90-252/394-3139; dinner for two XXX.

SHOP

Eski Sandik Boutique specializing in vintage hand-embroidered scarves and shawls. Yali Mevkii Atatürk Cad., 89/B Cami Sk., Türkbükü; 90-252/377-5497.

A suite's sitting room at Locanda al Colle, a boutique hotel in Tuscany, Italy.

chic sleeps

PURE SWEDEN

BY HEATHER SMITH MACISAAC
PHOTOGRAPHED BY MARTHA CAMARILLO

Hanging out
at Fabriken
Furillen, a
former cement
factory on
Sweden's
Gotland island.

Above: Enjoying
a coffee break
at a communal
dining table in
Stockholm's Hotel
Skeppsholmen.

of tuna tartare followed by tender slices of reindeer with lingonberry coulis (the food is all the more delectable for its isolated genesis). And there is drama—in spades. Heavy chains still hang from the ceiling of the former workers' canteen; they're no longer used, except as a superscale, necklace-like adornment. Large single-pane windows in the dining room frame a Charles Sheeleresque image of a hulking concrete tower next to a gargantuan heap of slag. There is a rugged, surreal, even romantic allure to the setting that the overcast sky only abetted, allowing all the subtle shades of gray to emerge. Like sound carrying across water, a woman in a bright orange jacket could be seen in the fog, sharp as a spark, way down the beach. One can only imagine the scenes Bergman, were he still filming, could have produced here.

But along with cinematic effects there is a degree of discomfort that comes from a slavishness to style: a small, handsome bar but no cozy lounge; poorly arranged, bare-bones bathrooms; no bedside reading lamps but instead an industrial fixture casting a hostile glare over the pillows. I felt at times like an interloper on a fashion shoot, moving amid a stylish young crew who are hospitable and earnest if not so experienced. Yet even interlopers have a fascination with the scene before them.

Fabriken Furillen is so unusual a place, one of such brutal beauty, that despite its refined faults, it stayed with me far longer than I stayed with it.

WAS I DREAMING? WAS IT THE LINGERING EFFECTS OF jet lag? Faintly, but as steadily as waves reaching shore, a chorus of shrieks lapped the window of my room at Hotel Skeppsholmen, in Stockholm. The cries, it turned out, were of false terror, erupting from the roller coaster at Gröna Lund—the capital's version of Copenhagen's Tivoli—a slingshot's distance across the water. Of all the sounds I had expected to hear at what is perhaps Stockholm's most central hotel, this had not been among them. The next morning, the breakfast terrace provided a more restful sound track: birds scuffling for crumbs; lanyards slapping against metal masts; the clink of cup finding saucer.

Like the still eye of a swirling storm, the isle of Skeppsholmen is a calm oasis in the center of Sweden's largest city. Yet it is not a hub. It is convenient enough that every section of the city is a mere walk, bike ride, or ferry trip away, but it is apart. The hotel itself is one of the few commercial enterprises on the parklike island, the others being a restaurant, a hostel aboard a 19th-century sailing ship, and two museums. None of them were going to contribute to disturbing the peace. Nor was traffic. Roads are few, cars even fewer. My taxi scarcely found the hotel in the dark, its signage was so minimal.

The discretion is fitting. Built in 1699 to house royal marines—the architect, Nicodemus Tessin the Younger, also designed the Royal Castle—the two 328-foot-long buildings are now protected as significant historic structures. Alteration is so restricted that when the hotel was created in 2009, any modifications needed to be reversible. I could as easily have been a midshipman returning to the barracks in the 18th century as a guest checking in, so little changed is the classic exterior—butter-yellow stucco walls; orderly rows of windows trimmed in gray; chimneys in strict formation atop dormered metal roofs, all in severest black.

Inside, in spite of the restrictions, the hotel steps fully into Scandi-modern mode. Sweden's architecture firm of the moment, Claesson Koivisto Rune, turned constraints into assets, emphasizing timeless materials such as wood and stone and adding dimension by playing with light and bursts of color. Punctuating the long corridors and stairwells like guiding beacons are outsize light installations by David Trubridge, Carola Lindh-Hormia, and Jameelah El-Gashjgari. In the 81 bedrooms, plain in the manner of a Jil Sander suit, the colors of the Swedish flag turn up in a bright-canary side table and small club chairs upholstered in soft blue. For bathrooms, the designers inserted stand-alone pods, all right angles save for the sensuous porcelain sinks modeled after skipping stones.

Luxury in Scandinavia is never obvious, lest it be mistaken for a French import. At Hotel Skeppsholmen it comes in the form of soaped pine floors smooth to the feet, Duxiana mattresses, duvets sheathed in crisp cotton, and body products from Byredo, an exotic yet made-in-Sweden line with graphics as chic and direct as the hotel's own. Down in the dining room, where the menu is limited but the quality is high, glass walls extend the shimmery effect of light bouncing off water, and a basket of sheepskins sits beside the door to the terrace, ready for use outside as seat cushions, baby blankets, or wraps when the wind picks up. In summer, you want to be outside as much as in, enjoying its greatest indulgences: the sea at your feet, quiet in your head, and the city all around you.

SKI AREAS IN SUMMER HAVE A LISTLESS, UNDER-LANDSCAPED quality. And that was my initial impression of Fjällnäs, a hotel in Malmagen, just northwest of the ski town of Tänndalen, on the Norwegian border. The wooden buildings—housing some 45 rooms, plus a hostel, spa, chapel, and main lodge—were unsheltered by vegetation, a bit exposed without their softening blanket of snow. This was my first trip to Härjedalen province—referred to by some as Southern Lapland, even though it's well below the Arctic Circle—and I was still adapting. The brightness of the red and yellow buildings was

familiar from the seven-hour drive through the countryside north from Stockholm; the topography was not. Sitting on glacial Lake Malmagen, Fjällnäs is surrounded by raw, rocky, windswept terrain shaped by ice 9,000 years ago. It made me feel both small and at the top of the world.

That a place so rugged, no matter how striking, would be the retreat of choice for well-heeled Stockholmers speaks volumes about Sweden's commitment to nature and appreciation for the fundamental. Guests have come to Fjällnäs since 1882, and the historic lodge is still the centerpiece of the resort, where one sits by the fire, maps out a cross-country-skiing route, and stokes up for the day on salmon, eggs, muesli, and strong coffee. It's also where hikers, cyclists, and families—often three generations' worth—unwind at day's end on the banquettes that line the dining room. Even in the cool daylight that accompanied dinner, everything glowed: the healthy faces and uniformly blond heads, the warm pine walls, the bright brass light fixtures that recall a similar model designed by Alvar Aalto in 1939.

Fjällnäs completed a smart renovation and redecoration in 2008. So along with the vintage postcard left on my pillow at night (from a long tucked-away stash found on the property) and the thick wool socks laid atop the blanket at the foot of the bed, there were Missoni towels and bathrobes in rich, narrow stripes. More stripes turned up in upholstered window seats and rag rugs lining a bench in the hall where one can sit down to change out of dirty boots. When it comes to highly refined practicality, Fjällnäs is pitch-perfect. Most bedroom floors are heated, as are towel bars. Each floor comes equipped with a drying closet for wet gear; each building has a vestibule generous enough to accommodate boots, skis, and all-terrain strollers.

Fjällnäs knows its audience: there is very little sitting around. In fact, the place empties out during the day, with guests taking off in all directions, not to be seen for hours. I joined them, accompanied by my friend Susanne, who had come prepared with caps and rucksacks. We added bottles of water to our picnic lunch, though the manager assured us we could drink straight from any stream. We hiked up a trail through mountain birch; despite its gentle climb, we emerged above the tree line onto a high plain of undulating rock tempered by scruffy vegetation. The scene was so vast, the vista so far and broad, as to be immeasurable. Only a wooden signpost gave any guidance or sense of scale.

Much as I loved my room at Fjällnäs, I could have lived at its Mii Gullo Spa. A scent that was a cross between balsam forest and wood smoke—pine tar, it turned out, used as a natural sealant for the building's wood cladding—set the scene. A fire burned in the lounge area. Funny elfin hats, to keep one's head warm outside post-sauna, and rough linen washcloths were stacked next to more of those colorful Missoni towels. A horizontal band of window in the sauna framed a panorama of lakeshore meeting mountain. Hardy Swedes moved nonchalantly from sauna to hot pool to a plunge in the frigid

From top:
Fjällnäs's
Mii Gullo Spa,
in Tänndalen;
a foliage-roofed
cabin at Urnatur
Skogseremitage,
in Ödeshög.

waters of the lake. I opted for a foot and lower-leg treatment called Kroktjärnen. Sitting in a chair while the therapist gently bathed my legs, I felt like a supplicant to a Norse god of well-being; I never wanted to leave. My mind wandered only so far as the magical setting I found myself in.

IF ONLY PEOPLE LIKE ULRIKA KRYNITZ AND HÅKAN Strotz had been in charge of the back-to-the-land movement of the 1960's. Hippies would have been heroes, communes would have had waiting lists, and environmentally, we'd all be way ahead of the game. The couple, a German and a Swede, did the opposite of dropping out: they got degrees in biology (Krynitz) and forestry (Strotz), traveled, studied, taught, designed, and then, in 1993, bought a farm in Ödeshög. And only naturally, very organically, did that farm develop into Urnatur Skogseremitage, an eco-reserve in green parlance, a summer camp for grown-ups in realspeak.

Three hours southwest of Stockholm on small Lake Visjö, Urnatur is like a demonstration model for the live-smart movement and a destination for those who wish to not so much turn back the clock as to slow it way down. In a place named for a Swedish phrase that means both "ancient nature" and "made from nature," everything that's in the woods is of the woods. From storm-felled trees, Strotz hand-built one main cabin, six guest cabins, two tree houses, and a bathhouse—the only structure with both electricity (solar-powered) and plumbing. (Strotz read the bibles of the American back-to-the-land movement, the Foxfire books from the 1970's, which inspired much of his craft and woodsmanship.) An apprentice constructed that most rare specimen, a delightful outhouse. Three of the cabins have roofs of peat and moss that spawn wild strawberries in late summer, and meld into a forest carpeted in plush, intense green. At Urnatur, nature and design dovetail seamlessly.

Pulling from Swedish, Amish, Shaker, Russian, and Japanese traditions, each cabin is unique but uniformly enticing. I wanted to stay in them all.

A 10-minute walk from the cabins, along a path bordered by pastures for Swedish heritage breeds of cows and sheep, brought me to the lake. Here, inside the "tin castle," a metal-roof building that's the largest at Urnatur, or on its deck, guests gather for conversation, a glass of wine, and Krynitz's fine meals, their ingredients pulled mostly from the farm. It was just before dinner, 8 p.m., and the sun was nowhere close to setting. I walked out onto a dock projecting into the lake. Calm waters mirrored a sky scattered with backlit clouds. It was hard to imagine a place more peaceful.

Urnatur is all fresh smells and new experiences and no rules—with the requisite do-it-yourself mentality. If you want crayfish for dinner, you can row out on the lake and check the traps with Strotz. Herbal tea? Forage on the grounds with Krynitz. When the sky finally darkens, you light your way with lanterns, your cabin with candles and kerosene lamps. After all, Strotz says, "What is more beautiful: a lightbulb or a burning candle?" When you want to bake in the sauna or stargaze from the hot tub, both part of the immaculate bathhouse, you dictate the temperature and advise Strotz, who stokes the fires that heat each.

Even taking into account their formal education, I was astonished by Krynitz and Strotz's knowledge—of carpentry and blacksmithing, of plant material and food and cooking, of animal husbandry, of Swedish history and lore, of current events and contemporary design, and simply of people. Here was a couple as attuned to human nature as to the natural world, quietly engaging hosts who knew when to step forward and when to pull back. Not just the creators and caretakers of Urnatur, they are its soul, making it a paradigm impossible not to want to emulate, impossible to replicate. ✚

resources

Fabriken Furillen Lärbro, Gotland; 46-498/223-040; furillen.nu; doubles from $$; open April–September.

Fjällnäs Malmagen, Tänndalen; 46-684/23030; fjallnas.se; doubles from $.

Hotel Skeppsholmen 1 Gröna Gången, Stockholm; 46-8/407-2300; hotelskeppsholmen.com; doubles from $$.

Urnatur Skogseremitage Sjögetorp, Ödeshög; 46-144/10234; urnatur.se; doubles from $, including some meals; open April–October.

AFFORDABLE HOTELS

Europe is filled with great places to stay that combine style and design with excellent value.
We've hunted down intimate, wallet-friendly lodgings in many of the Continent's most desirable cities and countryside
destinations. Here are a few discoveries worth a check-in—all for less than $250 a night.

Vienna, Austria

Old meets new at the 25-room **Hotel Hollmann Beletage** *(6 Köllnerhofgasse; 43-1/961-1960; hollmann-beletage.at; doubles from $)*, where the neo-Gothic 19th-century façade stands in stark contrast to the contemporary interiors: bold orange lamp shades and pillows; espresso-hued furniture; steel-wire chairs. Besides a prime location just steps from St. Stephen's Cathedral, the hotel's biggest standout is its eight-seat cinema, which screens Austrian films nightly.

Auvergne, France

High in the hills of Auvergne, a five-hour drive south of Paris, **Instants d'Absolu–Ecolodge du Lac du Pêcher** *(Lac du Pêcher, Chavagnac, Cantal; 33-4/71-20-83-09; ecolodge-france.com; doubles from $)* isn't for those seeking high-tech amenities or over-the-top service. *Calme*, on the other hand, is to be had in abundance: the farmhouse is surrounded by forested parkland. The 12 simple rooms are furnished with pine-wood tables and rough-luxe fabrics such as virgin wool, alpaca, and leather.

Athens, Greece

One of the world's most ancient cities has gotten a serious dose of high eco-style: the 79-room **New Hotel** *(16 Fillellinon St.; 800/337-4685; yeshotels.gr; doubles from $)* is the first property by noted designers Fernando and Humberto Campana, who are known for their cutting-edge use of sustainable products. Bamboo parquet floors, brass-clad washbasins, and asymmetrical workbenches forged from recycled materials are just a few of the hotel's environmentally friendly details.

Tuscany, Italy

Check all those rustic-charm expectations at the door of **Locanda al Colle** *(102 Via della Stretta, Camaiore; 39-0584/915-195; locandaalcolle.it; doubles from $)*, on the outskirts of Forte dei Marmi. Midcentury Danish and Italian furniture is punctuated by paintings and photographs from the 1940's to the present in the nine modern accommodations, which have taupe and green accents. The only thing quaint about the inn is the sweeping vistas of the Tuscan countryside.

Lisbon, Portugal

Once a watering hole for Lisbon's literati, the restored **LX Boutique Hotel** *(12 Rua do Alecrim; 351/213-474-394; lxboutiquehotel.com; doubles from $)* has been reborn as a sophisticated inn dedicated to Portuguese culture. Every level has a different theme, from the fifth-floor Barrio district, where rooms have graffitied walls, to the second-floor Fernando Pessoa, named for the 20th-century poet who penned some of his work at the property.

Glasgow, Scotland

Amsterdam-based CitizenM's third property, **CitizenM Glasgow** *(60 Renfrew St.; 44-141/404-9485; citizenm.com; doubles from $)*, made its debut with much fanfare in a city that has never had a reputation for contemporary digs. The boxy exterior looks more like a Jean Nouvel creation than the twee Scottish B&B that you typically find downtown. Public spaces are sprinkled with Eames chairs, and rooms include oversize beds and Philips "moodpads" to control the huge flat-screens and ambient lighting.

Andalusia, Spain

While rooms at the **Hotel la Fuente de la Higuera** *(Partido de las Frontones; 34/95-211-4355; hotellafuente.com; doubles from $)*, in the Andalusian mountains, are undeniably bare-bones (handcrafted antique furniture; dark-wood bed frames), the seven-acre property is all about *la buena vida*. Farm-to-table dinners are served at the outdoor restaurant each evening, and the shady pool is surrounded by large acacia trees. The region's fabled *pueblos blancos*—ancient whitewashed villages—are just a short drive away.

Istanbul, Turkey

Design aficionados love the 20-suite **House Hotel Galatasaray** *(19 Bostanbasi Cad., Beyoğlu; 90-212/252-0422; thehousehotel.com; suites from $)*, thanks to Turkish firm Autoban's makeover of the 1890's mansion. Polished parquet floors, marble staircases, and delicate moldings are set off by the subdued gray-and-taupe curtains and deep, velvet armchairs. Don't miss the snug penthouse lounge, with big leather sofas flanking a stone fireplace.

Clockwise from left: A bedroom in one of the suites at Italy's Locanda al Colle; a guest room at Instants d'Absolu, in France's Auvergne region; Istanbul's House Hotel Galatasaray; a lounge at Locanda al Colle; reading in the Play Room at Vienna's Hotel Hollmann Beletage; candy dispensers near the hotel's lobby; Instants d'Absolu's restaurant. Center: Greeting guests at Hollmann Beletage's front desk. Opposite: A stairwell in House Hotel Galatasaray.

Hotel Borgo San Felice, in Chianti. Opposite: The Galileo Room at Borgo Finocchieto, near Siena.

SCENES FROM ITALIAN VILLAGES

BY PETER JON LINDBERG
PHOTOGRAPHED BY MARTIN MORRELL

J

OHN PHILLIPS WAS ONLY LOOKING FOR A VILLA. THAT HE WOUND UP with a village says something about the scale of his enthusiasms, his impetuous streak, and the curious state of the Italian countryside at the beginning of the 21st century. But really, he insists: he never intended to buy the whole town.

For two years, Phillips, a prominent Washington, D.C., lawyer, had been scouting for a house in Tuscany. He'd begun his search in Chianti, but found little that suited his needs. Finally he turned his sights to the Val d'Orcia, 40 miles south of Siena. And there, in August 2000—on seven overlooked and overgrown acres that one might call the middle of nowhere, were not the famed wine town of Montalcino just 15 minutes away—Phillips came upon the tiny medieval hamlet of Finocchieto.

For two generations the hilltop farming village (whose name means "fennel fields") had lain abandoned and forlorn. At its pre–World War II peak Finocchieto counted 60 residents, mostly sharecroppers who worked the fields along the hillside. But postwar industrialization, coupled with agriculture's decline, led to a rural exodus across Italy, as farmers sought new work in larger towns and cities. Finocchieto's last holdouts moved away in the 1960's.

Opposite: Driving along the road to Castel Monastero, in Italy's Ombrone Valley.

What they left behind looked not so different from what their ancestors had known seven centuries earlier: a cluster of tiled-roof houses and farming sheds, connected by meandering footpaths, with a modest green and a courtyard at its heart. From the edge of the green the views stretched out for miles, across cypress-fringed pastures and vineyards and undulating hills. Finocchieto was, in short, an archetypal Tuscan village, or *borgo*, albeit in severe disrepair. By 2000 the footpaths were choked with weeds, the green turned to mud. Roofs had collapsed; trees were uprooted; the chapel was filled with rotting hay. Starlings nested in the 500-year-old communal brick oven where residents once gathered to bake the daily bread.

Phillips was undeterred. "The whole place was dilapidated, but there was such tranquillity," he says. "I'd never heard quiet like that. You could see it had amazing potential."

As was often the arrangement in rural villages, the former residents of Finocchieto did not own their property but rented from a landlord. The current owner was a wealthy signor who still lived in a castle just up the hill. Phillips made inquiries and learned that the man was prepared to sell—but he refused to break up the village. It was the whole *borgo* or nothing.

"So on my final day in Tuscany, in a fit of irrational exuberance, I decided to buy the entire thing," Phillips says, sounding bemused by his decision still. His wife, Linda Douglass, did not share this exuberance. "When Linda first came to see it, she began to cry," Phillips recalls. "Not tears of joy, but tears of 'What the hell were you thinking?'" Douglass now laughs at the memory. "It was as if my husband had gone to the store for milk, then came home to announce that he'd bought Safeway," she says.

But the deal was done, and now the question was what to do with the property. They certainly did not require an entire 300,000-square-foot village for a vacation home. Phillips began to conceive a grander role for Finocchieto: not quite a private retreat, not quite a hotel, but something in between.

THE IDEA OF TRANSFORMING DERELICT TOWNS INTO LODGINGS IS NOT NEW IN ITALY. IN FACT it was pioneered some 30 years ago, by a tourism marketing consultant named Giancarlo Dall'Ara, as

a means of rehabilitating a struggling village in Friuli. Dall'Ara's notion was to convert the village's empty apartments and houses into B&B-style lodgings, independently owned but managed as a collective. Guests would eat their meals in town, interact with residents—for some villagers did remain—and play out the age-old traveler's fantasy of living like a local. Dall'Ara called the concept an *albergo diffuso*—a "diffuse" or "scattered" hotel. (His Friuli project, called Albergo Diffuso di Comeglians, is still in operation.)

Since then, scores of abandoned or near-abandoned Italian towns have been reimagined as village hotels. The Associazione Nazionale Alberghi Diffusi, of which Dall'Ara is president, now counts 48 member properties across the country, with dozens more taking shape. Meanwhile, the Swedish-Italian hotelier and philanthropist Daniele Kihlgren has raised the bar with his Sextantio brand, creating hardcore-authentic *alberghi diffusi* out of a 15th-century mountain village in Abruzzo and, even more impressive, inside the Sassi di Matera cave dwellings in Basilicata. (Kihlgren has acquired nine more sites across southern Italy, which await similar transformations.)

Ironically, the economic stagnation that nearly decimated so many Italian villages in the 20th century wound up saving them for the 21st. Mired in poverty, passed over by modern development, they were essentially suspended in time. In a country whose celebrated hill towns are commonly littered with Vodafone signs and Benetton shops, this is a welcome outcome indeed.

And the *albergo diffuso* turns out to be a sustainable model for both development and preservation. Repurposing existing structures costs less, and has a smaller carbon footprint, than constructing new hotels. *Alberghi diffusi* create jobs for area residents and, if they source products locally, help sustain traditional crafts and trades. They also pass along much of the cost of preservation to a demographic that strongly benefits from it: travelers. That last part is crucial. Tourism is often blamed, sometimes accurately, for reckless and degrading development. But under the *albergo diffuso* rubric, tourism becomes an agent for preservation, providing both the catalyst and the capital. And hotels, rather than overwhelming the historic fabric, can form an integral part of it.

WHAT'S REMARKABLE IS HOW MANY OF THESE ghost villages still exist in Italy, ripe for the remaking—untold hundreds, emptied out by rural flight and barely touched, or noticed, in the decades since. This, in one of the most well-charted and tourist-trafficked landscapes on earth.

The secret is out. More and more wealthy buyers are acquiring defunct villages as their own private vanity fiefdoms. Not surprisingly, many of these latter-day doges—call them the *borgolomaniacs*—are from overseas: Americans, Koreans, Russians, Japanese. But *borgo* fever has swept the home country as well. Rare is the Italian designer who hasn't accessorized with a village. Alberta Ferretti bought up the tiny hamlet of Montegridolfo, in Emilia-Romagna. Brunello Cucinelli took over most of the Umbrian village of Solomeo. And Massimo Ferragamo spent several years—and undisclosed millions—turning the medieval *borgo* of Castiglion del Bosco, just downhill from Finocchieto in the Val d'Orcia, into an extravagant resort and residential complex.

Ferragamo's is the most over-the-top entry in a variant breed of village hotel, which takes the same humble setting but ramps up the luxury quotient. Examples can be found across the Continent: from Castelnau des Fieumarcon, a fortified Gascogne village that became a 33-bedroom retreat, to Aman Sveti Stefan, a Montenegrin hamlet turned hotel, care of Amanresorts.

Still, Italy is the nexus of the *alberghi diffusi* movement, and a good number of them are in Tuscany. One of the high-end pioneers of the trend—and still among the most convincing—was Hotel Borgo San Felice, which occupies a 1,300-year-old church and settlement in Chianti, 13 miles northeast of Siena. Converted to a hotel in 1979, and now a Relais & Châteaux property, it makes clever (re)use of original village details: street names and address numbers were left intact, while restaurants and shops are marked with old-fashioned signage.

A short drive away, in the Ombrone Valley, the Castel Monastero resort began life in A.D. 1050 as a monastery. Developers retrofitted the 13 original buildings with 75 guest rooms, a private villa, a wellness center and spa, an art gallery, and—apparently just because they could—a Gordon Ramsay restaurant. Rubelli fabrics, rough-hewn timber beams, worn terra-cotta floors, and faded 19th-century frescoes set a mood of carefully rusticated opulence. Of course, Castel Monastero and its ilk are missing a key component of the traditional *alberghi diffusi*: actual villagers. Giancarlo Dell'Ara's original model in Friuli was set in a still functioning (if struggling) village, with which it was and remains interdependent. Other properties continue to follow

that example. Physically speaking, the best *alberghi diffusi* may retain the integrity of their traditional townscapes and historical details. But without their original residents—without giving guests the sense of being in a community, surrounded by everyday people and not just hotel staff—a village hotel risks feeling like a conventional resort.

The other risk is that they wind up fetishizing the rural life, selling a sanitized brand of peasant chic. A genuine village stay, after all, would not be nearly so restorative: those crumbling stone floors wouldn't be swept and polished just-so, the bathwater might be only lukewarm, and *nonna*'s handwoven blankets might not be so artfully arranged on the bed. But for many, the implication of authenticity is still preferable to none at all. And few things can make a world-weary mogul feel better about himself than a week spent pretending he's a 13th-century shepherd. Especially if he still gets turndown service.

FOR JOHN PHILLIPS, IT TOOK TWO YEARS OF negotiations with Italian authorities before he could begin to restore Finocchieto. The renovation itself, overseen by a local architect (with Phillips flying in every few months), took another five years. Strict local preservation laws

forbade changes to the footprint or contour of the buildings—all exterior walls and fenestrations had to remain as they were. Where structures had deteriorated or collapsed, they were rebuilt according to the original village plans, which are archived at the local preservation office.

Certain interior adjustments were allowed. "The second story of the main house was on all different levels, so we had to raise and lower floors and ceilings," Phillips says. "Here and there we reconfigured staircases, shored up ceiling beams, and unbricked archways to increase flow and light." Ultimately, 22 bedrooms would occupy the *borgo*'s five buildings: nine in the main house, five in the smaller house, four in the chapel, and two in each of the former storage sheds. Bathrooms were updated, but not overly so. (The guest directory devotes two whole pages to plumbing instructions.) Each of the four outbuildings has its own kitchen, dining, and living room; in the main house are two dining rooms, a parlor, a library with a vaulted ceiling, a cantina for wine tastings, a banquet and conference hall, and a brand-new, retro-modern kitchen.

From the outside, however, the *borgo* looks pretty much as it does in the sepia-toned photographs displayed in the library—albeit with tidier lawns. Footpaths were

Above, from left: Castel Monastero's piazza; the bocce court at Borgo Finocchieto.

The Piano Room at Borgo Finocchieto. This page, clockwise from right: Borgo San Felice; Borgo Finocchieto's swimming pool; the hotel's chef, Luigi Ricci, and his wife, Chantal.

A fruit salad at Castel Monastero. This page, clockwise from left: The hotel's spa; Ricci's fettuccine at Borgo Finocchieto; harvesting olives on-site.

relaid with flagstones; flowerbeds were planted with lavender, rosemary, sage, and thyme, which perfume the breeze that slips over the hills. All the functional anachronisms—the air-conditioning system, the laundry, the 18-car garage—have been concealed underground. A sleek gym and spa were cleverly tucked into the hillside behind a nine-foot wall of glass, out of the sight lines of the village above. The swimming pool and tennis and basketball courts are likewise hidden down the hill. Stand on that manicured green, squint, and you might believe this is still a working village.

Borgo Finocchieto officially opened in spring 2008, and has since operated mainly by word of mouth. Word passed quickly. The exuberantly social Phillips knows approximately half the population of Washington, D.C., and Douglass, a former ABC News correspondent, likely knows the rest. In one hallway is a framed note from Teddy and Vicky Kennedy, who visited the *borgo* in 2006, in the midst of renovations. Alice Waters, another friend of Phillips, is Finocchieto's unofficial culinary consultant.

While it has the services and polish of a luxury resort, including a full-time staff of nine, Borgo Finocchieto is not a conventional hotel. The target clientele is not so much independent travelers (though individual bookings are welcome) but groups, who might book a single house or even the entire village. Phillips anticipates a mix of celebratory gatherings (family reunions, birthday or anniversary parties) and high-minded retreats (academic conferences, educational programs, think-tank summits). Ultimately he sees the *borgo* becoming "a place for culture, arts, food, music, policy, and ideas," on the model of, say, the Aspen Institute—or, for that matter, the American Academy in Rome, of which Phillips is a trustee. "This place

works so well in bringing people together, even people who didn't know each other beforehand," he says.

That was certainly the case during my visit. The *borgo* was near-full, giving it the lively air of a proper village. At traditional country resorts, one's instinct is to seek out a private corner and keep to oneself, but at Finocchieto an easy communal feeling prevailed. For all the time and money spent on renovations, the *borgo* maintains a remarkably unpretentious, even homey, feel; there's a softness, a worn-ness to the place that can only come from centuries of everyday use. The crowd that weekend was a balance of hotel guests and a few old friends of Phillips. My wife and I knew not a soul among them, but within a few hours of arriving we were bonding over a rowdy 12-person bocce tournament. We all lingered long over breakfasts on the terrace—oven-warm cornetti, prosciutto di Parma with melon from the garden—then went our separate ways in the afternoons, biking, touring wineries, visiting Siena or Montalcino. At sundown we reassembled for communal dinners in the main house, under forged-iron candelabras and ceiling beams the size of tree trunks. Luigi Ricci, the *borgo*'s chef, who spent 20 years working with Paul Bocuse, conjured great rustic feasts of Cinta Senese, Chianina steaks, luscious house-made mozzarella, and pappardelle with rabbit *ragù*.

Alice Waters herself happened to be at the *borgo* that weekend as well. On our final Sunday she was inspired to clear the cobwebs from the 500-year-old oven, gather some olive-wood kindling, and fire up some note-perfect crostini with ricotta and honey. We devoured it while sitting on the lawn, gazing out over the shimmering fields of the Val d'Orcia, then settled in for one last postprandial round of bocce. There are worse afternoons. ✚

resources

Albergo Diffuso di Comeglians Comeglians, Udine; 39-0433/619-002; albergodiffuso.it; doubles from $.

Borgo Finocchieto Bibbiano, Siena; 202/657-6828; borgofinocchieto.com; suites from $$$$$ per night, including breakfast, three-night minimum.

Castel Monastero Monastero d'Ombrone, Siena; 39-0577/570-001; castelmonastero.com; doubles from $$$, including breakfast.

Castiglion del Bosco Montalcino, Siena; 39-0577/191-3001; castigliondelbosco. it; doubles from $$$$, including breakfast.

Hotel Borgo San Felice Castelnuovo Berardenga, Siena; 800/735-2478; borgosanfelice.it; doubles from $$$, including breakfast.

La Galatea In the historical center of a small Apulian town only a few miles from the Ionian Sea. Galatone, Lecce; 39-333/678-4170; albergodiffusolagalatea. com; doubles from $.

Sextantio Via Principe Umberto, Santo Stefano di Sessanio, L'Aquila; 39-0862/899-112; sextantio.it; doubles from $$, including breakfast.

Sextantio Le Grotte della Civita 28 Via Civita, Matera; 39-083/533-2744; sassidimatera.com; doubles from $$.

SPOTLIGHT
A PARIS LEGEND

In late 2010, Philippe Starck revamped Le Royal Monceau-Raffles Paris. Steps from the Champs-Élysées, the hotel embodies a glamorous, artistic sensibility that rivals the Ritz, the Crillon, the Meurice, and the Plaza Athénée. Here, all the details behind the perennial enfant terrible's most sophisticated work to date.

THE STYLE

Built in 1928, the unapologetically luxe hotel now has a keen sense of modernity. In the public spaces Starck laid down a custom-designed carpet with an intricate tree-branch motif and set out a mix of furniture pieces ranging from Arne Jacobsen's 1958 Egg Chair to a polychromatic hand-beaded seat from Africa that looks like a small throne. Lower-profile but no less welcome are the streamlined sofas, ottomans, and side tables where guests and visitors relax over drinks in Le Grand Salon, the lobby area. There is also that enduring Starck favorite, a long communal table, adjacent to the bar.

THE INTERIORS

"It is all about 'inhabited' rooms," Starck says. "I tried to imagine the rooms of creative, cultured, elegant people. But most of all, I blurred the style." The 149 suites are a welcome mix of furniture and lighting, carpets and fittings, an eclectic fusion of talent. You'll find Murano glass lamps and classic Milanese designs from the 1970's, as well as white stone-topped oval tables with polished-metal pedestal bases that are reminiscent of Eero Saarinen's 1956 Tulip collection. "They are full of a feeling, a spirit, a presence, as if someone invisible is welcoming you," Starck says. To that end, underneath the glass that tops the wooden desks in each suite, a map of Paris has been annotated with must-see spots highlighted by the designer himself.

THE AMENITIES

The bathrooms are extraordinary feats of precision. White on white, with polished steel fixtures and glazed doors—some translucent, others transparent—that open to the oversize shower, the WC, and the walk-in closet, they feature blindingly radiant ceilings that take the form of a grid, with a rheostat to control the megawatt lighting. In lieu of terry-cloth slippers in the closets—which are modeled after the private *cabines* in couture houses— Starck specified French canvas espadrilles. Overscale mirrors, leaned nonchalantly against guest-room walls, turn into televisions at the flip of a switch.

THE RESTAURANTS

For **La Cuisine**, helmed by executive chef Laurent André, contemporary artists hand-painted porcelain plates, for which Starck created tall vitrines that line one side of the dining room. A glass wall faces a garden where trees, shrubs, and herbs grow. Starck personally selected the photographs and prints that adorn the walls, and artist Stéphane Calais painted

La Cuisine's white ceiling with a simultaneously subtle and sprightly mix of shapes and colors that recalls the work of Alexander Calder. There is a smaller, Italian restaurant, **Il Carpaccio**, which Starck envisioned as part grotto, part solarium—with seashells embedded in the walls, ceiling, and chandelier.

THE EXTRAS

A cigar bar, **La Fumée Rouge**, is lined in bordello-red leather panels and looks out onto a glazed wall of individual humidors that look like safe-deposit boxes in a bank vault. Off Le Grand Salon is a wood-paneled bookstore stocked with some 700 art publications. **Le Spa My Blend by Clarins** includes an 85-foot-long subterranean pool. Next door is the hotel's exhibition gallery and, adjacent to the lobby, there is a private screening room, Le Cinéma des Lumières, that features 99 oversize leather chairs modeled after a first-class airplane section; 98 of those seats are dove gray, while one, arbitrarily situated among the others, is lipstick red.

Le Royal Monceau–Raffles Paris 37 Ave. Hoche, Eighth Arr.; 800/768-9009 or 33-1/42-99-88-00; raffles.com; doubles from $$$$$.

Clockwise from above: A guest bathroom at Le Royal Monceau; the hotel's entrance; Le Cinéma des Lumières screening room; an annotated map of Paris; a Philippe Starck–designed chair in a suite; oversize lighting in La Cuisine restaurant; Le Grand Salon, the hotel's lobby; Starck's espresso cups; Domoina de Brantes, the hotel's art concierge. Center: The cigar bar, La Fumée Rouge.

AN IRISH MANOR REBORN

BY CHRISTOPHER MASON
PHOTOGRAPHED BY JOHN KERNICK

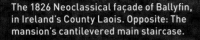

The 1826 Neoclassical façade of Ballyfin,
in Ireland's County Laois. Opposite: The
mansion's cantilevered main staircase.

SET IN THE FOOTHILLS OF THE SLIEVE BLOOM MOUNTAINS IN County Laois, 60 miles southwest of Dublin, the Neoclassical mansion of Ballyfin was erected in 1826 to trumpet the wealth and prestige of Sir Charles Coote, Premier Baronet of Ireland. When the Coote family fell on hard times after World War I, the estate was sold for a measly £10,000 and became Ballyfin College, a boys' school run by Catholic monks who were unable, or disinclined, to manage its upkeep. After decades of neglect, the property was in a pitiful state of disrepair. Delicate plasterwork in the Gold Drawing Room had been destroyed by seeping rainwater when its current owner, Fred Krehbiel, a Chicago-based businessman, first visited in 2000.

After 40-odd years of global peregrinations as an executive at an electronics corporation, Krehbiel and his Irish-born wife, Kay, were tempted to dip their toes into the hospitality trade. "I felt it would be interesting and fun to find an old property we could turn into a small hotel," said Krehbiel, an earnest, square-jawed Midwesterner of Swiss descent, when I paid a visit to Ballyfin last winter, five months before its scheduled opening in May. As we warmed ourselves by the hearth in the Saloon—a butter-yellow reception hall with Corinthian columns and a pair of gilded mirrors designed by Robert Adam and made by Thomas Chippendale—Krehbiel explained that his vision was to "re-create the feeling of staying in a very grand Irish house where comfort is the key ingredient."

In doing so he appears to have taken to heart the punning family motto of the builder, the ninth baronet Coote: *Coûte que coûte,* or "Cost what it may." Millions were expended on Ballyfin's lavish restoration—Jim Reynolds, the Irish landscape designer recruited to oversee the entire project, was reluctant to specify a figure. He would acknowledge only that the estate was acquired in 2002 for €7 million, a matter of public record. "That's the only number we remember," Reynolds told me in his salty Irish brogue, roaring with laughter at my impertinence for asking about costs. "There never was a budget," he insisted. "We did what had to be done."

THE RENOVATIONS PROVED A BOON TO THE LOCAL ECONOMY, PROVIDING EMPLOYMENT TO more than 200 workers, including visiting specialists. Conservation experts examined the mansion's crumbling sandstone façade and determined that 60 percent of the stone needed to be replaced—a two-year project in itself. A 500-foot-long underground tunnel was installed, running from the estate's 18th-century stables to the mansion's basement, so as not to blight the pastoral landscape with commercial vehicles. The tunnel helps create the illusion of inhabiting a paradise unconnected to life's daily grind.

"The idea was that you lived in an ideal world, free of care and travail," Reynolds said. "Nothing will go through the front door but the guests and their bags." The hotel accommodates a total of 29 guests, who are attended to by a full-time staff of 40.

Of the 15 guest rooms and suites, one of the more fanciful is the Westmeath Bedroom, named after Marianne, Countess of Westmeath, whose portrait, by the studio of Sir Thomas Lawrence, hangs above the fireplace. (Her extracurricular exertions in a carriage with the Honourable Augustus

Opposite, clockwise from top left: Conservationist John Harte, who helped restore the mansion's inlaid floors; afternoon tea service in the Gold Drawing Room; the Stair Hall's antique suit of armor; the estate's 18th-century grottoes.

Opposite:
Ballyfin's
Sir Christopher
Coote Suite.

Cavendish-Bradshaw inspired one of the most scandalous divorces of the 1790's.) The room is dominated by a carved French bed with a domed canopy of cream silk tethered to a gilded frame.

Krehbiel invited the current baronet, Sir Christopher Coote, to visit Ballyfin, with the hope of learning more about the estate's history. After seeing the American's plans to restore the estate, Coote offered to sell Krehbiel 17 of his family portraits so they could again grace the walls of Coote's ancestral home. The portraits are now installed in the Stair Hall, an ornate space with turquoise walls and a cantilevered staircase. Visitors are met by the flinty stare of the armor-clad Sir Charles (1581–1642), a soldier-adventurer and the first Coote to set foot in Ireland; his "prominent and excellent military service" earned him a baronetcy from James I in 1623. "By all accounts he was the most rapacious and murderous individual," Reynolds said. "His reputation was worse than Cromwell's."

Subsequent generations of Cootes were more congenial. In the grand entrance hall is a splendid Roman floor mosaic brought back from a Grand Tour taken by the ninth baronet and his wife, Lady Caroline, a niece of the Earl and Countess of Meath.

During my visit in January, afternoon tea—a sumptuous affair with fruitcake and raspberry jam—was served in the library, an 80-foot-long room with a fireplace at either end. A bow window in the center offered a glorious view of a grand Italian marble fountain, lined up with the center of the window. When the Krehbiels first saw it, the fountain was two feet off center. "Someone said, 'You shouldn't move it. It's so wonderfully Irish,'" Reynolds told me. "But Fred is Swiss," he added drily.

To the left of a fireplace, a hidden door behind a bookcase swings open to reveal a spectacular curvilinear glass-and-steel conservatory with Roman statuary, wicker furniture, and potted palms. Neglected by the monks, the frame was severely corroded and had to be dismantled and shipped, piece by piece, to England for restoration. Meryl Long, a recent visitor, remembers her father, Richard Guinness, describing his astonishment at finding bananas growing in the conservatory in the early 1920's—an almost inconceivable luxury in Ireland at the time.

Alas, Reynolds has no plans to revive the cultivation of bananas. But he has planted a kitchen garden to produce fresh vegetables. And he has introduced free-range chickens to supply eggs. The hotel's chef, Fred Cordonnier, was previously in charge of Restaurant Patrick Guilbaud at the Merrion hotel, Dublin's only Michelin two-starred restaurant; at Ballyfin he will apply his French technique to the local bounty, whether a porcini risotto with slices of Jerusalem artichoke or tender lamb from the Slieve Bloom mountains.

And then there are the grounds. Ballyfin sits on 600 acres, with a vast lake in front of the house and a network of diverting walkways to a rockery with ferns, all modeled on the style of Lancelot "Capability" Brown. Outdoor activities include boating and fishing; tennis; bowling; croquet; and bicycling on more than six miles of paths. Beyond the property's 4½-mile stone-walled perimeter, there is horse trekking, as well as outings to Birr Castle, with its famous arboretum and gardens, and the Lutyens gardens at Heywood, in Ballinakill. The Heritage golf course, designed by Seve Ballesteros, is 20 minutes away.

Will Krehbiel's spectacular gamble pay off? With Ireland's economy still in disarray, Ballyfin will have to look abroad for much of its clientele. That said, the hotel's central location—halfway between Dublin and Shannon—makes it an ideal stopping point for travelers bound from the capital to the southwest coast.

"We're certainly not going to get a return on our investment," Krehbiel said, though he betrayed not a hint of regret. ✚

resources

STAY
Ballyfin Co. Laois; 353-57/875-5866; ballyfin.com; doubles from $$$$$, including all meals.

DO
Birr Castle Demesne Stately gardens on the grounds of a 17th-century castle. Birr, Co. Offaly; 353-57/912-0336.

Emo Court Neoclassical estate and gardens built in 1790 by architect James Gandon. Emo, Co. Laois; 353-57/862-6573; open 10 a.m.–6 p.m., April through September.

Heywood Gardens Ballinakill, Co. Laois; 353-57/873-3563; open daily, year-round.

Rock of Dunamase Limestone ruins that date back to an A.D. 842 Viking settlement. Between Portlaoise and Stradbally, Co. Laois; open daily, year-round.

Bakers from Amedeo
Giusti with their
house-made focaccia,
in Lucca, Italy.

food & drink

Seafood-and-
vegetable soup
at Nauthóll,
a bistro in
Reykjavík,
Iceland's capital.
Opposite:
The primeval
landscape of
Snæfellsnes.

FARM TO TABLE IN ICELAND

BY SHANE MITCHELL
PHOTOGRAPHED BY CHRISTIAN KERBER

O N A CHILLY AUGUST MORNING IN EASTERN ICELAND, a herd of reindeer paused to graze along a granite ridge. Eymundur ("Eymi") Magnússon, a dead ringer for the Bee Gees' Barry Gibb, slammed on the brakes, and his truck skidded to a halt on the stony track. The two of us sat silently watching as these skittish herbivores, their enormous antlers swaying like velvet chandeliers in a windstorm, trotted toward a glacial lake outside the town of Eglisstaðir.

"Do they know you don't eat meat?" I asked.

Magnússon chuckled. "Maybe. Hunting season is coming up soon, and they've been on my land for most of the summer."

Surveying the matted crowberry shrubs and lichen-crusted rocks, I didn't see much terrain that could be construed as sanctuary for creatures that stuck out like a frost giant's sore thumb. But once we bounced around several turns in the rutted trail, the truck dipped into a hidden vale of barley fields. The wind died away as we drove between tall rows of mature aspen.

Magnússon remarked at the curious hue of the sheltering foliage, possibly tinted by nitrogen from blue lupines blooming underneath. "No one thought these trees would grow," he said, "but I have planted one million of them." In a forestless realm where all virgin timber was cut down more than a thousand years ago, it's an achievement worthy of a vegetarian visionary. For Magnússon, who supplies tiny white potatoes and fruit preserves to gourmet shops in Reykjavík, it was simply another day on the farm he calls Vallanes.

JUST KISSING LATITUDE 67 DEGREES NORTH, THIS ISOLATED ISLAND OF VOLCANOES AND glaciers is what the Icelandic people have called home—literally between hot rocks and a cold place— since A.D. 874, when their intrepid Viking ancestors first rowed longships across the Norwegian Sea. Unlike its nearest neighbor, Greenland, Iceland is warmed by the Gulf Stream, so the climate is relatively temperate. Although summer is fleeting on the cusp of the Arctic Circle, plenty still grows here, and Icelanders are champion foragers of mushrooms, berries, moss, seaweed—anything deemed remotely edible. Word about these rare ingredients, not to mention the weird beauty of an untamed landscape, has spread far beyond the island's lava-rock shores. Danish chef René Redzepi, the leader of the New Nordic culinary movement and an avid forager, sources Icelandic seafood, herbal teas, and the yogurt-like skyr for Noma, his Copenhagen bistro, which in 2010 was named the world's top restaurant (edging out Spain's El Bulli) by a prestigious international food academy.

These modern-day Vikings can cite an ancient literary source for their foraging instincts: the Icelanders' sagas, which are filled with heroic deeds by poet-farmers and warrior-shepherds. I've never managed to choke through an entire narrative, but undoubtedly the Old Norse words for *locavore* and *sustainability* are in there somewhere.

I share a love of scrounging with these far northerners. My mother, an early convert to the health-food craze during the 1960's, favored Euell Gibbons's *Stalking the Wild Asparagus* as her

Opposite, clockwise from top left: Eygló Ólafsdóttir and Eymi Magnússon on their farm, Vallanes; the Gufufoss waterfall; salmon on a bed of slate with organic Icelandic flowers and skyr at Dill, in Reykjavík's Nordic House; the Hótel Aldan, in Seyðisfjörður.

guide to walking on the wild side. She taught me to be an edible opportunist, hunting the sides of streams for cress and picking windfall apples from abandoned farm fields near my childhood home. My own inspiration, however, is an obscure gem titled *Icelandic Picnic,* by Áslaug Snorradóttir and Sigrún Sigvaldadóttir. Full of tart homilies, this merry collection of arty snapshots celebrates the outdoor pleasures of a brief yet bountiful season, when modern Vikings pack their camping gear and plunder the countryside with berry buckets. At the height of an Arctic summer, I also discover how short a distance it is in Iceland to journey from field to table.

IN A TIE-DYED BUNKHOUSE ON MAGNÚSSON'S farm, a group of WWOOF-ers were wolfing down wild-blueberry pancakes and rhubarb compote. World Wide Opportunities on Organic Farms is a grassroots cultural exchange for back-to-the-land volunteers and growers eager to embrace the crunchy gospel. This crew ranged from a Bowdoin graduate student researching soil content to an elderly Englishwoman with a passion for tundra fungi—all extra hands in the farm's prized potato patch. "Don't let anyone in Reykjavík know they're ready to harvest yet," Magnússon entreated me. *Icelandic*

Picnic: "*Þjóð veit, ef þrír vita.*" "If three have been told, the whole nation knows."

With packets of freshly baked angelica-seed crackers from Magnússon's wife, Eygló, in my bag, I left the gentle vale of Vallanes for a rough gravel road to the nearby eastern seaport of Seyðisfjörður. As I gained elevation, the weather closed in. I found myself navigating a suspension bridge with a dense cloud bank underneath and zero visibility in a region where free-ranging sheep mobbed grassy shoulders. Halfway through my route, the Gufufoss waterfall tumbled over a series of rock terraces next to the road. I parked and walked to the edge, where the spray misted my face and hair. One of the most wonderful things about Iceland is the purity of plain old tap water, which tastes of minerals from the sunless halls of mountain kings.

Seyðisfjörður was preparing for a midsummer party. A heap of broken furniture and packing crates piled next to the town hall was to be torched at sunset—which, at this time of year, was just shy of midnight. At the reception area in the Hótel Aldan, the old checkout counter displayed iced fruitcakes and chewy nut cookies; oak tables and Windsor chairs looked out onto the waterfront. Setting my place with a crocheted doily

and candlestick, a waitress recited the evening menu. (Magnússon's microgreens made an appearance, paired with a smoked duck breast.)

As I watched bonfire-bound townspeople stream past the front window, succulent langoustine tails arrived garnished with Gotland truffle foam. Closer in size to crawfish than lobster, Icelandic *humar* are rich enough on their own. The sauce made from mushrooms sourced on a Baltic island was an indulgent embellishment, particularly given the frugal culinary history of a people who once survived winters on putrefied shark and pickled seal flippers. *Icelandic Picnic: "Margt er sætt í dag, sem súrt er á morgun."* "Sweet today, sour tomorrow."

AN EIGHT-HOUR DRIVE AWAY, THE CAPITAL OF Reykjavík has all the hallmarks of a small college town—street murals; vintage stores; Internet cafés. I was there to meet Siggi Hall, an ardent fan of Magnússon's potatoes. Tall and jolly, Hall is the Icelandic equivalent of the Galloping Gourmet; he introduced his viewers to imported comestibles such as olive oil and maple syrup, but now promotes a cooking philosophy closer to home.

We met for langoustine chowder at Nauthóll, a modern bistro overlooking the city beach. I asked him what a summer picnic means to an Icelandic chef. "I like to go out to the country with blankets and sandwiches, smoked lamb, and cheeses," he said. "Especially in August, when the berries get ripe. Everyone has their secret picking grounds." He leaned in closer to stage-whisper: "You don't tell where you pick your berries!"

Set in grassy parkland on the outskirts of town, Nordic House was designed by Finnish master architect Alvar Aalto. The minimalist structure holds a library and exhibition space. It is also home turf for two culinary madmen. By day, Dill restaurant serves as the museum cafeteria; after hours, all that changes radically. Chef Gunnar Karl Gíslason and his sommelier, Ólafur Örn ("Óli") Ólaffson, produce poetry from an experimental kitchen slightly smaller than a bread box. Gíslason may just be the next René Redzepi. Because Dill has only 10 tables, each plate gets his conceptual scrutiny, and what winds up on that rustic china is extraordinary. Often Gíslason will hear from a lone hunter who has bagged a reindeer, or a former Buddhist monk who combs the shoreline for kelp and moss. Arctic char might arrive from friends who have spawning streams flowing past their sheep paddocks. A ceramic artist will trade dinner for a pot

Above, from left: Bread and cider-vinegar butter at Dill; dining on the terrace at Hótel Aldan. Opposite, from left: Puffin with cabbage, parsley purée, and stout crackers at Hótel Búðir, on the Snæfellsnes Peninsula; staffers at Reykjavík's Kaffismiðja Íslands.

of protruding lamb bones. And a waiter's uncle supplies fresh-mown hay for one of Gíslason's quirkier pairings.

The meal required a wicked sense of humor enhanced by a capacity for surprise: I had never seen pickled green wild strawberries, birch oil, caramelized cheese whey, or pink beer. The cubed, salt-preserved wild salmon with capelin roe and smoked-rapeseed mayonnaise tasted like fishy Pop Rocks with a nicotine twist. A loin of Icelandic beef, cooked rare, was dusted with incinerated leeks. (At one point I spotted Gíslason setting fire to a clump of hay outside; the ash fell on a breast of wild goose.) Magnússon's potatoes nestled next to scrambled duck egg and bacon in cream sauce. A dollop of whipped cider-vinegar butter perched precariously on a lava rock next to pumpernickel. When the kitchen finally closed and Gíslason pulled up a chair, I asked him why he scorched his food. He crossed his meaty arms and grinned like a garden gnome. "For extra grill flavor," he said, laughing.

FORAGING IS A PURSUIT EMINENTLY SUITED TO THE road, and all the better if that byway winds around fjords leading to the Snæfellsnes Peninsula. Every few miles I stopped to scan for fragrant thyme and stalks of seeding angelica. The trip to Hótel Búðir, a country house on the Atlantic—usually a 2½-hour drive northwest from Reykjavík—took me most of a day. After a brisk walk along the pebbled beach to gather mahogany kelp washed up at low tide, I rinsed the sea salt from my hands in an upstairs guest room and headed to the dining room to settle onto a tufted banquette.

Búðir's owner and chef, Petur Thordarson, sources much of his menu from farms on the peninsula, with a few exceptions. I was intrigued by the gamy flavor of his seared puffin with parsley purée. Accompanying the buttery lamb fillet and pulled shank: a mound of Magnússon's barley. (Was there no escaping this agricultural activist?) I couldn't resist begging some wild cèpes, which smelled like chocolate from a bog.

The windows faced west toward Snæfellsjökull volcano, which some here consider a vortex—an energy point where the earth's magnetic core supposedly attracts supernatural phenomena. My waiter casually mentioned that in winter the aurora borealis seems to arch closer to it. Even in summer, snow caps this mystic cone, the setting for the start of the fictional expedition in Jules Verne's *Journey to the Center of the Earth*.

On my last morning, the Búðir kitchen gave me a two-gallon plastic bucket. The lane leading back to the main road passed through a dormant lava field blanketed by soft mosses. I hiked among the jumbled rocks and climbed down into a wide crevice out of the wind blowing off the ocean. All around me were low bushes full of plump blueberries that no one had yet found.

I picked and picked. Sitting there on the dry grass, with the sound of the surf at my back and the glacier sparkling in the sun above me, I finally had a taste of that transient delight relished by a Nordic race of alfresco revelers. *Icelandic Picnic: "Nú er af mér gengið, sagði geitin, ég er bæði full og feit."* "Now I'm done, said the goat, I'm both full and fat." ✚

Opposite: The dining room at the Hótel Búðir.

resources

STAY

101 Hotel Modern, art-focused property with 38 rooms. 10 Hverfisgata, Reykjavík; 354/580-0101; 101hotel.is; doubles from $$.

Hótel Aldan Comfortable, traditional inn and restaurant on the waterfront. 2 Nordurgata, Seyðisfjörður; 354/472-1277; hotelaldan.com; doubles from $; dinner for two ✗✗✗.

Hótel Búðir Iceland's finest country hotel; rooms look out on a tidal inlet or a glacier. Búðir Snæfellsnes; 354/435-6700; budir.is; doubles from $; dinner for two ✗✗✗.

Vallanes Working barley farm with accommodations for traveling members of WWOOF. Eglisstaðir; 354/899-5565; vallanes.net; doubles from $.

EAT

Dill 5 Sturlugötu, Reykjavík; 354/552-1522; dinner for two ✗✗✗.

Kaffismiðja Íslands The city's best coffeehouse. 1 Kárastígur, Reykjavík; 354/517-5535; coffee for two ✗.

Nauthóll Bistro 106 Nauthólsvegur, Reykjavík; 354/599-6660; lunch for two ✗.

SHOP

Frú Lauga Icelandic Grocery and gift shop that sells fresh local produce, artisanal cheeses, and fruit preserves from Vallanes farm. 20 Langalækur, Reykjavík; 354/693-7165.

SOHO RESTAURANTS

Depending on the Londoner you ask, Soho's "renaissance" has been simmering for anywhere from 20 years to 60. But now the simmer has reached a rolling boil, as some of Britain's most venerated chefs and savviest restaurateurs have set up shop in a few square blocks of the West End. Here, the cream of the crop.

Wright Brothers Soho Oyster House

The sister establishment to Borough Market's favored oyster bar is a bigger, sleeker, and cannier affair than its sawdusty sibling. It's spread across multiple levels, with several bars and extensive table seating. Subway tiles and brass candlesticks gleam with the patina of expensive design. The menu focuses on *fruits de mer* and English staples (smoked mackerel; Cornish crab with brown bread; fish pie), which are executed nearly flawlessly. In few places does breaded and fried calamari achieve such subtle flavor. Some 30 affordable wines and a formidable gin selection round out the picture. 13 Kingly St.; 44-20/7434-3611; dinner for two ✖✖✖.

Gauthier Soho

Chef Alexis Gauthier commandeered this Georgian town-house site, laid on the heavy linen and ornate silver in its airy dining rooms, and opened it as a starchy French restaurant, with a Michelin star and a minimum three courses, served in one sitting nightly. But his sublimely fresh meat and produce combine thrillingly, with an emphasis on surf-and-turf pairings: quail is married to smoked eel under a light cèpe sauce, while Dover sole finds depth in a meat-and-citrus *jus*. 21 Romilly St.; 44-20/7494-3111; dinner for two ✖✖✖ .

Bocca di Lupo

With an open, brightly lit industrial kitchen ringed by a generous bar lined with tall leather stools, Bocca di Lupo has drawn dense, boisterous crowds since it opened in 2008. Chef Jacob Kenedy turns out flavorful twists on Italian classics. Musts include the shaved-radish and celeriac salad tossed with pomegranate, pecorino flakes, and truffle oil; and the crunchy-crisp, outrageously fatty suckling pig on a bed of sautéed *cime di rapa*. (Gelupo, right across the road, is Kenedy's *gelateria*; its offerings are similarly delicious, with flavors that change daily.) 12 Archer St.; 44-20/7734-2223; dinner for two ✖✖✖ .

Hix

Chef Mark Hix's cachet transcends location—he could open a snow-cone stand in Basingstoke and the masses would come—but his Brewer Street boîte is at the nexus of the Soho action. In a former sushi bar (out with the lacquered screens, in with the Home Counties whitewash), an amiable staff that's erudite in all things locavore brandishes trays of Whitstable Native oysters and cuts of Langley Chase organic lamb for your approval. Even the fish fingers have a provenance worth extolling. Dishes read a bit precious on the menu, but arrive as simply prepared perfection. And yes, that's Tracey Emin in the corner. 66-70 Brewer St.; 44-20/7292-3518; dinner for two ✖✖✖.

Polpo and Polpetto

Russell Norman, the ex-operations director of Caprice Holdings restaurant group (the Ivy; J Sheekey; Le Caprice), opened Polpo in 2009—a paean to tin-ceilinged, filament-bulb-lit Lower East Side hipsterdom. The menu is succinct and printed on your paper place mat; the *cicchetti*—crostini of asparagus, Taleggio, and prosciutto; apricot-studded rabbit terrine—come cheap and tasteful, courtesy of an alarmingly cool waitstaff. Polpetto is Polpo in miniature: 12 tables housed above the storied French House pub. Whichever you choose, order yourself a *quartino* of Barbera d'Alba and settle in for the inevitable, but worthwhile, wait. Polpo: 41 Beak St.; 44-20/7734-4479; dinner for two ✖✖. Polpetto: 49 Dean St.; 44-20/7734-1969; dinner for two ✖✖.

Clockwise from top left: Head chef Jai Parkinson in London's Wright Brothers Soho Oyster House kitchen; the restaurant, housed in a former rectory; Bocca di Lupo's roast suckling pig with grapes; the zinc-topped bar at Hix; Gauthier Soho's Georgian façade; bottles of I Tre Borri Chianti at Bocca di Lupo; roast pork belly served with radicchio and hazelnuts at Russell Norman's Polpo; one of the restaurant's embroidered curtains. Center: A bar overlooking the open kitchen at Wright Brothers.

Bicycles parked outside Amedeo Giusti, a traditional bakery in Lucca, Italy. Opposite: A view of the city from Guinigi Tower.

A TASTE OF TUSCANY

BY GARY SHTEYNGART
PHOTOGRAPHED BY DAVID CICCONI

Renaissance-era walls seem quite happy with the jewel-box approach. And yet, we all crave surprise. Lucca is known for its churches, among them the 11th-century wedding cake of San Michele in Foro and the San Martino Cathedral, its sacristy containing Jacopo della Quercia's magnificent Gothic tomb of a poor young dear who died in childbirth, her dog loyally roosting by her feet. But three months after my visit these images are relegated to quick postcard snaps on my phone. The only interior that still echoes in my mind is the Basilica di San Frediano. Not for its simple Romanesque proportions or its relative humility, but because in the sullen emptiness of one afternoon a middle-aged procession of just-off-the-bus Germans with their rolling luggage still behind them unexpectedly take over one of the chapels and, under the guidance of their skinny, polyester-clad pastor, suddenly raise their voices to God.

I'VE COME TO LUCCA TO VISIT FRIENDS, AND TO EAT. Shilpa and Antonio live in the peaceful villa district of Monte San Quirico, across the river from Lucca. For Italy they are an unexpected couple. Antonio's background is half Lucchese and half Piedmontese (which might as well

be foreign around here), while Shilpa is Indian American. Antonio's politics are center-right, Shilpa's the opposite. Their frequent disagreements about the quality of pale, white, salt-free Tuscan bread are operatic, hilarious, and instructive. In a nutshell, a staple that to Antonio may represent identity, resilience, and Tuscan thrift, to Shilpa represents some pretty bad bread. Meanwhile, their son Zubin, a brown-eyed five-year-old, reminds us of his favorite nursery rhyme ("O is for Obama"). After a few hours with Shilpa and Antonio's family, the Kebab Controversy and the reign of the Northern League begin to seem slightly abstract.

The first place we hit for sustenance lies outside of Lucca's walls. What's even more shocking for wine-soaked Italy is that we are headed for an award-winning brewery by the name of Birrificio Brùton. Inside this cavernous repurposed farmhouse, next to a sweet terrace filled with jazz and children, a waiter sporting sideburns and leather bracelets heats up a jar of baby food while stroking the cheek of a mesmerized youngster. Iacopo Lenci, the 27-year-old owner, serves serious beer and formidable pub grub. Lenci's dad is a winemaker, which brings to mind both continuity and rebellion. We're quaffing large amounts of Brùton's notable Dieci beer, so named for its 10 percent alcohol content, a magnificently fruity creation endowed with notes of caramel and licorice, as well as the chocolaty Momus, which somehow stacks up against the kitchen's pig shank with sauerkraut, juicy grilled onions, and a hamburger (yes, a hamburger!) composed of rich Tuscan meat and a familiar sesame-seed bun. The bun instigates another discussion on the quality and provenance of Tuscan bread, during which Shilpa says of Lenci and his groundbreaking brewery, "This guy's the future of Italy. This is the only way it'll go forward." No one disagrees.

Our next stop: a restaurant named Grano Salis, also outside of Lucca's walls. Firouz Galdo, an Iranian-born architect working in Rome, was brought in to create a contemporary space full of light, wood, and pewter—the whole thing could easily sit atop a Hong Kong skyscraper. Grano Salis, packed with young locals, is certainly in the pro-kebab camp. Its website weighed in on the controversy, noting that Italian cuisine is flooded with foreign influences and that there's not a whale of difference between, say, sashimi and crudo or, for that matter, kebabs and the Italian spiedini. The interior of Grano Salis is covered in mottoes such as MANGIA COME PENSI ("Eat like you think"), and thoughtful is the best way to describe the restaurant's professional and knowledgeable waitstaff, who will say things like: "The octopus we saw today at the market was too small. We didn't like it."

What they *did* like were the succulent mini-clams in the ramen-thick, beyond-al-dente *tonnarelli con polipetti e pecorino* and the silky *trippa* of *baccalà alla romana*, sitting atop tomato and garlic on toast. We drink down a Tenuta delle Terre Nere, grown in the rocks of the Etna volcano, with an aromatic complexity that boggles the mind and leads to comments along the lines of "The filthiest wine I've ever had" and "It tastes like a very dirty child."

Another night, we go to Ristorante Lombardo, in the pretty hills of Santo Stefano, 15 minutes outside of Lucca's walls. Lombardo specializes in very honest Lucchese cuisine, such as the stewed codfish with leek, and also represents some decent and inexpensive local wines. Facing the port of Livorno, the restaurant's terrace feels temperate and joyous with nuclear families, the mountains nearly glisten, and the lack of light pollution is spectacular. The egg-yellow *tortelli*

lucchesi are a meaty double threat—there's beef and pork and bread crumbs inside, and beef and pork (and tons of vegetables) in the sauce. Lombardo's pillowy specimens are so rich, eating them feels like biting into a Swiss franc.

IT'S TIME TO HEAD DOWN TO THE CITY. THE WALLS, built for defensive measures but never used as such, are perfect for an evening stroll, forming a kind of raised expressway with handy exits. By sundown the parapets are overrun with chirping teenagers, industrious joggers, picnickers enjoying golden focaccia by the battlements, and any people who think they are in love. I commute along the north side to the Palazzo Pfanner, a hydrangea-scented refuge abutting the walls, and the most geometrically lovely spot in Lucca, a copse of bamboo reaching up to the San Frediano bell tower. Within the space of a half-hour, I traverse the length of the city to find Lucca's gem of a botanical garden, where an 1820 Lebanese cedar provides tall comfort. To build an appetite I do some browsing at Antica Gioielleria Carli, the famous jeweler along the Via Fillungo. Forgive what I said earlier about jewel boxes, because that's precisely what Carli is, with its hushed, private air, its 17th-century vault, its bright frescoes, and its outstanding collection of silver, watches, and unusual objects such as Neapolitan *corni* (horns), amulets carved out of red coral that are imputed to ward off the evil eye.

Tonight's dinner is at Trattoria da Giulio, an airy, pleasantly undistinguished space smack-dab by the walls. Shilpa and I sample a heavy and chewy *zuppa di farro* that clearly benefits from the use of only the best grain and that inspired Shilpa's mom, on a previous visit to da Giulio, to proclaim it every bit as flavorful as *khichdi*, the Indian national comfort dish. Somewhere out there, the Northern League is not pleased.

The next day I circulate hungrily within the city walls. At the touristy but still vital Buca di Santantonio restaurant, I lunch on a grilled fat-ribboned baby goat cooked on the spit along with an artichoke pudding that holds, but does not entomb, the complex, salty flavor of artichoke. For dinner, I lean back at Ristorante All'Olivo's outdoor terrace, which is seductively shrouded in bougainvillea and the aromas of a superior kitchen. I partake of a langoustine that might as well be butter, amazing red mullet, fatty raw oysters, and

Buca di Santantonio's beef-and-pork tortelli. Clockwise from above: A canal in Livorno; the tea room at Palazzo Pfanner, in Lucca; copper pots in Buca di Santantonio's dining room.

Cacciucco, a seafood stew, at Trattoria l'Antico Moro, in Livorno. Clockwise from below: Antica Gioielleria Carli, a jewelry shop on Lucca's Via Fillungo; the Palazzo Pfanner; the entrance to Trattoria l'Antico Moro.

Opposite:
Outdoor seating
at Pult Drink
& Food, on
Lucca's Piazza
dei Mercanti.

a sauce of balsamic, oil, pepper, salt, and, yes, fellow kebab-defenders, soy.

But the best restaurant within the city walls for my euro is Pult Drink & Food, centrally located in the Piazza dei Mercanti on the Via Fillungo. The staff here is as talkative and knowledgeable as the crew at Grano Salis: "I wouldn't get that bottle first," the waiter says. "It's a little too insistent and powerful." He steers us instead to an expansive Ribolla Gialla from Friuli. The owners used to have a popular shack by the sea and now they've gone big in the city, creating an outdoor summertime oasis favored by up-to-date locals—everywhere you look you'll spot those famous Lucchese schnozzes buried tide-deep in fish. We feast on the red mullet and scampi so typical of nearby Livorno, and sweet shrimp that bring to mind Japanese *ama-ebi*. Pult has the best crudo in town, which is saying something, and nicely salted and olived sea bass. The *fritto misto* is ethereal, particularly the zucchini and shrimp; indeed the art of frying at Pult is deft and Japanese. The only warning: During late nights in summer, a terrifying dance party may break out.

THIS TALE ENDS FAR OUTSIDE LUCCA, IN THE SEASIDE city of Livorno. A short train ride away, tourist-free Livorno is everything Lucca is not. Flattened by Allied bombs, lacking any must-sees except for some canals in the so-called New Venice district and a church featuring, forgive me, one of Vasari's ugliest paintings, Livorno nonetheless manages to thrill because of its diversity. The port city was once home to Italy's largest community of Jews living outside of a ghetto and some of these free-range Jews are still in evidence, along with churches bearing Armenian, Dutch, Anglican, and Greek Orthodox affiliations. In addition to the slightly corroded sea air, I've come to sample Livorno's famous dish, *cacciucco*, at Trattoria l'Antico Moro, a seafood restaurant that smells entirely like its wares. *Cacciucco* is one of several local dishes that have Jewish origins, a metaphor for multicultural Livorno. The fragrant stew is an amalgam of at least five different kinds of fish, made from whatever the fishmonger has on offer, set afire by liberal use of red pepper, enhanced by tomato and red wine vinegar and plenty of toasted garlic bread. With its array of dismembered sea creatures, a flotilla of fish tails peeking out, a distinctively non-Jewish langoustine hiding underneath, *cacciucco* looks like an underwater Battle of the Somme. It is the messiest dish I've ever seen or eaten, and it burns my stomach, ears, and eyes in a way that is memorable and real. After the studied perfection of Lucca's cuisine, I am happy to live in a world where muddy fish stews can exist a short train ride away from heaps of golden *tortelli lucchesi*, where kebabs are cheap and plentiful, and where a simple Tuscan *farro* soup can remind an Indian mother of home. ✚

resources

STAY

Locanda l'Elisa Quiet inn minutes from central Lucca. 1952 Via Nuova per Pisa; 39-0583/379-737; locandalelisa.it; doubles from $.

Locanda S. Agostino Bed-and-breakfast in a 15th-century villa. 3 Piazza S. Agostino; 39-0583/443-100; ocandasantagostino.it; doubles from $.

EAT

Birrificio Brùton 5135 Via Lodovica, San Cassiano di Moriano; 39-0583/579-260; dinner for two ✗✗.

Buca di Santantonio 1/3A Via della Cervia; 39-0583/55881; dinner for two ✗✗✗.

Grano Salis Via Dante Alighieri; 39-0583/190-0093; dinner for two ✗✗.

Pult Drink & Food 42 Via Fillungo, Piazza dei Mercanti; 39-0583/495-632; dinner for two ✗✗✗.

Ristorante All'Olivo 1 Piazza San Quirico; 39-0583/496-264; dinner for two ✗✗✗.

Ristorante Lombardo 4801 Via della Pieve Santo Stefano; 39-0583/394-268; dinner for two ✗✗.

Trattoria l'Antico Moro 27 Via Bartelloni, Livorno; 39-0586/884-659; dinner for two ✗✗✗.

Trattoria da Giulio in Pelleria 45 Via delle Conce; 39-0583/55948; dinner for two ✗✗.

DO

Antica Gioielleria Carli 95 Via Fillungo; 39-0583/491-119.

Botanical Garden 14 Via del Giardino Botanico; 39-0583/442-160.

Palazzo Pfanner 33 Via degli Asili; 39-0583/954-029.

San Frediano Basilica Piazza San Frediano.

San Martino Cathedral Piazza San Martino.

San Michele in Foro Church Piazza San Michele.

FOOD MARKETS

European markets are ideal places not only to shop but also to eat. Whether you're after mouthwatering pasta in Sicily or barrel-tapped sherry in Madrid, food just tastes better from a kiosk, eaten on a bench surrounded by a riot of produce. Below are our picks of the Continent's most vibrant mercados, marchés, and bazaars.

LONDON
Borough Market
Crammed with stalls, pubs, shops, and small restaurants, Borough Market is grazing central in London. Come early on Thursday or Friday and avoid the Saturday crush. *8 Southwark St.; 44-20/7407-1002; boroughmarket.org.uk.*
BEST BITES At the outdoor grill operated by **Brindisa** *(Middle Market; sandwiches for two ✗)*, the smoky chorizo-and-arugula sandwiches on crusty ciabatta rolls are worth the wait. Or indulge in seared scallops on a bacony bean-sprout stir-fry from **Shellseekers** *(Middle Market; scallops for two ✗)*, whose owner dives for the mollusks himself. For dessert, there's rich St. Lucian chocolate from **Rabot Estate** *(2 Stoney St.; dessert for two ✗)*.

MADRID
Mercado de San Miguel
Housed in a 1916 Beaux-Arts building, San Miguel market stood abandoned for years—until a renovation in 2009 gave it a new lease on life. Now it's a lively destination with 38 shopping and dining stalls, plus a central café area. *Plaza de San Miguel; mercadodesanmiguel.es.*
BEST BITES Sherries drawn straight from the barrel are accompanied by Andalusian olives and roasted nuts at **El Yantar de Ayer** *(#22-25; snacks for two ✗)*. **Pinkleton & Wine**

(#68-71; drinks for two ✗) offers some two dozen sparkling wines by the glass—just right with the *fines de claire* oysters from bivalve and caviar purveyor **Daniel Sorlut** *(#67; oysters for two ✗)*.

PARIS
Marché des Enfants Rouges
Besides trading in colorful produce and lusty charcuterie, this *petit marché* (one of the city's oldest) in the Marais is the spot for an affordable meal assembled from a diverse collection of ethnic prepared-food stands. *39 Rue de Bretagne, Third Arr.*
BEST BITES La Rôtisserie Enfants Rouges *(33-1/42-78-43-15; lunch for two ✗)* serves up crisp-skinned Bresse chicken with potatoes and a glass of *vin rouge*, while **Le Traiteur Marocain** *(33-1/42-77-55-05; lunch for two ✗)* is a must for its bracing spiced lamb-and-prune *tagine* and fluffy *couscous royale.*

PALERMO, ITALY
La Vucciria
It doesn't get more raucous than Palermo's labyrinth of narrow passages, where feisty matrons haggle with vendors in thick Sicilian dialects for the best pomegranates or tangy Pantelleria capers. *Between Corso Vittorio Emanuele and Via Roma.*
BEST BITES *Pane c'a meusa*, the unexpectedly tasty spleen

sandwich sold at almost every stall, is a Vucciria initiation rite, but the squeamish can opt for addictive *panelle*, puffy chickpea fritters. Snag a seat at the old-school **Vecchia Trattoria da Totó** *(5 Via Coltellieri; 39-333/315-7558; lunch for two ✗✗)*, which draws a crowd of regulars for its *pasta con sarde* (pasta with sardines) and convivial owner, Enzo.

ISTANBUL
Grand Bazaar (Kapali Çarşi)
With more than 4,000 shops spread out over 65 covered streets, Istanbul's 15th-century bazaar is *the* place to stock up on kilims and 24-karat bangles. Naturally, the army of vendors need to be fed, hence the delicious food finds. *Kalpakçilar Caddesi and Çarsikapi Nuruosmaniye Caddesi; 90-212/519-1248; kapalicarsi.org.tr.*
BEST BITES Goldsmiths, rug lords, and copperware kings pack into **Subaşi** *(48 Çarsikapi Nuruosmaniye Caddesi; lunch for two ✗✗)* for white beans in tomato sauce and chicken stuffed with rice. To sample the ultimate meat wrap, grab a *döner* at **Dönerci Şahin Usta** *(Nuruosmaniye 7 Kiliçilar Sokak; lunch for two ✗)*, near the Nuruosmaniye Gate. At the Cebeci Han caravansary, **Kara Mehmet Kebap Salonu** *(92 İç Cebeci Han; kebabs for two ✗)* serves the city's best kebabs.

with these early ripening varieties

Blenheim Orange
- quite sweet, crumbly texture, good with cheese
£2·70 per kg

Cox's Orange Pippen
- Spicy, honeyed nutty & pear like
£2·70 per kg

Clockwise from top left: Cutting swordfish at Sicily's La Vucciria; the market's artichokes for sale; food stalls in Madrid's Mercado de San Miguel; Meeting Point butcher shop; London's Borough Market, under Victorian railway arches; Turkish snacks at the Grand Bazaar, in Istanbul; the bazaar's vaulted alleys. Center: Bins of apples at Borough Market.

A WEEK IN
THE RHÔNE VALLEY

BY BRUCE SCHOENFELD
PHOTOGRAPHED BY ANDREA FAZZARI

Grenache grapes at Château de Saint Cosme, in Gigondas, France. Opposite: La Verrière, an inn and winery in Crestet.

THE LUNCH MENU AT L'OUSTALET IS SIMPLE, A FEW LINES scrawled on a chalkboard. There's roast chicken or turbot with vegetables, a green salad or rabbit pâté as a starter, an apple tart for dessert. Here in the wine lands of the southern Rhône Valley—those manicured slopes, limestone outcroppings, and picture-book towns that knit the river to the west to the Alpine foothills toward the east—such limited selections are de rigueur these days. Restaurants take a curious pride in how little they have to offer, since creating a midday prix fixe only out of what has caught the chef's attention at the *marché* that morning will keep food fresh and costs down. Locals can return day after day without growing weary of the options.

L'Oustalet sits on the main square in tiny Gigondas, half an hour north of Avignon. It has firm chairs of dark leather, crème-brûlée walls, and a 21st-century sensibility, from the informality of the sommelier to the clean, colorful plates of food set beside the bottles of wine (for everyone is drinking at lunch) on the plain wooden tables. And isn't that Louis Barruol from Château de Saint Cosme, my favorite area producer, sitting in the corner? Gigondas is pretty as a picture, a riot of bright shutters and doors, shady plane trees, stone walls and barrel-tile roofs, well-stocked gourmet shops and wine bars, and flowers everywhere, but it's also a working wine town. It hasn't stopped in time like the Provençal villages on the other side of Avignon that can seem as static as Monets.

This is the heart of French wine country, which is both a physical reality and a state of mind. My view, past the tables and out the door to the bright sunshine, is pretty much what most people are imagining when they book a trip to France to eat and drink well, spend their days surrounded by beauty, and perhaps visit a winery or two. And that's exactly what I was looking to do when I planned this weeklong vacation with my family: Find somewhere that made the fantasy of an idealized French wine trip come to life.

I've been to most of France's wine regions and enjoyed them all. But Champagne is formal, Burgundy can be inhospitable and imposing to an outsider, and Bordeaux is a collection of historic buildings on a flat, uninspiring landscape. The Rhône is different. The wine itself is hearty, unfussy, the kind you want to drink first and think about later. The landscape is glorious, a lavender-tinged segue of the Alps into Provence. And the towns on the hillsides and in the valleys have an authenticity that can only come from functionality. "They have a heartbeat," said Nicole Sierra-

Opposite: A table set in the garden at Carpentras's Maison Trévier, a hotel in an 18th-century town house.

Above, from left: La Verrière's Olive Grove room; chef Raoul Reichrath prepares squab at Le Grand Pré. Opposite, from left: Harvesting at a vineyard in Gigondas; owner Gina Trévier in the library of Maison Trévier.

Rolet, who runs a working winery and a country retreat called La Verrière in the hills above Crestet, just northeast of Gigondas. "They're real. They have festivals and bakeries and gossip."

A New Yorker raised in Italy, Sierra-Rolet left a high-powered banking life for a second act in wine country. (Her husband, Xavier Rolet, CEO of the London Stock Exchange, flies in on weekends.) Her husband had picked the area around Gigondas, she told me, because it "ticked all the boxes." I thought of that as we explored the region day after day, through villages such as Châteauneuf-du-Pape and Vacqueyras, Rasteau and Cairanne, that I knew from the wines that bear their names. Each seemed a perfectly composed backdrop, with its tidy square and post office and *boulangerie* and precisely painted storefronts, yet I never felt that any of it was being staged for our benefit.

Instead, we delighted in eavesdropping on real life, eating at bistros among the shopkeepers and doctors and businessmen, watching them pick out produce at the market, kicking a soccer ball with their kids. We were experiencing that bustle and hum of daily existence that

we all know well enough, but as played out in a most appealing setting. There wasn't a postcard in sight.

ALL RIGHT, IT WASN'T ALL QUITE AS PROSAIC AS THAT. One night, sitting outdoors by a gurgling stream at Le Moulin à Huile, in Vaison-la-Romaine, we ate truffle omelettes with foie gras cooked by Robert Bardot, who once served as the private chef for Frank Sinatra. Another night, we drove to Le Grand Pré, a restaurant where squab, a staple of area menus, is composed into something resembling art. Roasted to a perfect crimson, glazed with caramelized soy sauce, and placed atop a bed of red rice with two slices of blood sausage, it was a dish infinitely subtler and lighter than it sounds, and almost too pretty to eat.

At Crillon le Brave, a tiny hilltop town, we stayed at the Relais & Châteaux property of the same name, a dramatic hotel of gardens and terraces and glorious views. We spent several days pitching *boules* and gazing down at the vineyards and lavender-covered hills that stretched to the horizon. Because I love wine, I visited a few producers. But my wife and two sons stayed

behind at the hotel, and they seemed to be enjoying the trip as much as I was.

And that's a hallmark of wine country, a sense and sensibility you'll find from Sonoma to the Greek isles. It's always a grape-growing area, of course—and the wine made from those grapes needs to be renowned enough to be part of the area's identity. But it's also a place where wine's particular virtues have been incorporated into the prevailing mind-set. Wine is convivial; it draws people together, at restaurants and cafés and at home. Yet at the same time, wine is contemplative. You can't spend much time around it, or the vines that produce it, without considering some grander philosophical concepts in the seasonal rhythms of growing and harvesting grapes and the artisanal labor of transforming them into something beyond mere juice.

I felt those rhythms even in loud, chaotic Carpentras, where we spent our first few nights. Ideally positioned to explore the area, it's the hub of a wheel that encompasses Châteauneuf-du-Pape, Vacqueyras, Gigondas, and Vaison-la-Romaine. You wouldn't call Carpentras pretty, yet it has glorious aspects. It's

multicultural, with its Turkish restaurants and Tunisian bars and shops selling incense and fezzes and Indian spices, but one afternoon I took a walk and landed on a wooden bench outside a music school, where I heard a violin lesson through an open window. The scene was so quintessentially Gallic that I felt like I'd gone back half a century, to when the only language you'd ever hear on those streets was French.

I'd booked us a room at Maison Trévier, a town house dating from the mid 1700's that sits in the midst of the shopping district. We ended up occupying the entire middle floor, which includes a kitchen and a vast sitting room decorated with impressive-looking oil portraits that could have hung in the provincial museum down the street. Gina Trévier, the granddaughter of a grape grower, had owned a wine bar in Paris for 15 years but came south in 2005, she said, for a healthier lifestyle. I understood what that meant after she prepared us dinner: a salad of spinach, fresh fava beans, and olives, then stewed duck with turnips and carrots.

I awoke the next morning to the sound of happy voices from below. My boys were already downstairs

Opposite: The
pool at Hôtel
Crillon le Brave.

in the garden, shaded from the warm morning sun by a canopy, reveling in a singular breakfast of fresh bread smeared with organic apricot and quince jams that Trévier had preserved the previous fall, a semi-savory cherry cake, and homemade cherry juice. "When you find good wine," she told us as the birds chirped, "you will always find good food and a nice place to stay." I hadn't imagined that my wine-country fantasy would include quince jam and cherry juice miles from any winery. Yet when I look back now, that morning captured the essence of the trip as much as any wine-soaked dinner or picturesque drive.

ON ONE OF OUR LAST MORNINGS, I SET OUT ALONE for Gigondas and Château de Saint Cosme. Châteauneuf-du-Pape is the southern Rhône's most famous wine, but I actually enjoy Gigondas better, and Saint Cosme's most of all. Gigondas itself is higher and cooler than Châteauneuf, and unlike its neighbor, its soil isn't studded with shiny stones that serve to radiate heat and reflect the sun up into the vines. As a result, the grapes in Gigondas don't get nearly as ripe, and the wines are able to show a litheness, a nimbleness, that the thicker and more powerful Châteauneufs lack.

The wines Louis Barruol makes are serious, to be sure, yet deliciously refreshing, which is a trick that only a few producers anywhere in the world are able to manage consistently. I found him sitting at his desk surrounded by rugby paraphernalia. We talked about history, and geology, and family, all of which were in his mind inexorably intertwined, then set off to see the property. Soon we were climbing the hill toward a 12th-century chapel that sits beside the vineyards. I glanced up to see the Dentelles de Montmirail—the spiky limestone rocks that constitute the most recognizable geological feature of this area—looming against a sky of otherworldly Provençal blue, and Barruol's words from earlier echoed in my brain. I understood what it meant to have 14 successive generations of your family produce something from the local soil. It made me appreciate the wines that much more.

Later, we tasted in the second-century cellar, reputedly France's oldest. In the 2007 Le Poste, I noticed the flintiness of the region's limestone. The Le Claux, sourced from vines planted in 1875, had a floral nose and high tone that reflected the slope of the vineyard and the crispness of September mornings. I could taste the idea of wine country in every sip, the gathered wisdom of all those generations of Barruols in every glass.

Soon we said our goodbyes, and as I emerged into the bright day, with the Dentelles over my shoulders, I realized that it was noon and I was hungry. There was no question what to do next: I turned my car toward L'Oustalet and lunch. ✚

resources

STAY

Hôtel Crillon le Brave Place de l'Église, Crillon le Brave; 33-4/90-65-61-61; crillonlebrave.com; doubles from $$.

La Verrière Chemin de La Verrière, Crestet; 33-4/90-10-06-30; laverriere.com; doubles from $$.

Maison Trévier 36 Place du Docteur Cavaillon, Carpentras; 33-4/90-51-99-98; maison-trevier.com; doubles from $.

EAT

Le Grand Pré Rte. de Vaison-la-Romaine, Roaix; 33-4/90-46-18-12; dinner for two **✕✕✕✕**.

Le Moulin à Huile Quai Maréchal Foch, Rte. de Malaucène, Vaison-la-Romaine; 33-4/90-36-20-67; dinner for two **✕✕✕✕**.

L'Oustalet Place du Village, Gigondas; 33-4/90-65-85-30; lunch for two **✕✕**.

TASTE

Château de Saint Cosme La Fouille et les Florets, Gigondas; 33-4/90-65-80-80; saintcosme.com; open Monday–Friday 9 a.m.–5 p.m.

Domaine de la Janasse 27 Chemin du Moulin, Courthézon; 33-4/90-70-86-29; lajanasse.com; open Monday–Friday 8 a.m.–noon and 2 p.m.–6 p.m.; during harvest and weekends by appointment only.

Pierre Usseglio Traditional Châteauneuf producer on a picturesque hill. Rte. d'Orange, Châteauneuf-du-Pape; 33-4/90-83-72-98; open Monday–Friday, 9:30 a.m.–noon and 2 p.m.–6 p.m.

SHOP

Carré Boutique A smartly designed shop selling tapenade, olive oil, flavored salts, and other regional specialties. Place de la Fontaine, Gigondas; 33-4/90-62-31-42.

Characters dressed
in 17th-century garb in
front of the Hermitage,
in St. Petersburg, Russia.

style & culture

VENICE MADE EASY

BY VALERIE WATERHOUSE
PHOTOGRAPHED BY MARTIN MORRELL

Crossing the Piazza San Marco.
Opposite: Gondolas tied up along
the Grand Canal.

My

FIRST ENCOUNTER WITH VENICE, AS A SMALL CHILD, WAS A WHIRLWIND OF CANDY-COLORED palazzi, delicate blown glass, and narrow streets where you could get lost for days. There was also a spectacular procession of black gondolas, each bearing mountains of flowers, floating down a canal—part of the funeral, it turned out, of the great composer Igor Stravinsky.

Venice has always known how to honor its past. It's the present—and future—that have proved more unwieldy to negotiate. Today, the city manages to defy being characterized as a historical amusement park, one that's sinking—literally and metaphorically—under the weight of its history. Witness the controversial pedestrian bridge by Santiago Calatrava that spans the Grand Canal. Or François Pinault's contemporary art center, designed by Tadao Ando. Yet despite these changes, Venice remains, as always, committed to its past. Organizations such as Venice in Peril, Venetian Heritage, and Save Venice are leading efforts to make sure the city's treasures are preserved for future generations. Step into even the smallest of printing or woodworking ateliers, and you'll find craftsmen working just as they would have generations ago. And while the lesser-known side of the city sometimes surprises visitors, the legendary hotels and landmarks are what lure them back.

For years, the grand hotels around the Piazza San Marco have had few rivals. There are two Starwood Luxury Collection properties: the 16th-century Hotel Gritti Palace, residence of the former Duke Andre Gritti, and the revamped Hotel Danieli, which now houses 225 stylish rooms. Then there's the Bauer Il Palazzo, with its splendid terrace bar, the Bar Canale; and, of course, the legendary Cipriani, whose gardens alone justify the trip to neighboring Giudecca Island.

But along with these, a host of intimate properties are worth a look. Opposite the Church of the Frari, in the city's historic center, lies the discreet town house–style hotel Oltre il Giardino. Beyond a wooden door, a narrow path leads you through a brick-walled garden full of magnolia and olive trees to a stylish six-room villa. Owner Lorenzo Muner has furnished the space with family heirlooms and antiques, including 18th-century oil paintings and a framed vintage Gucci scarf. For art lovers, there is the regal Ca' Sagredo, a 42-room palazzo dating back to the 15th century, where 18th-century Rococo master Pietro Longhi's *The Fall of the Giants* flanks an elaborate marble stairway at the entrance. The room to book is Suite No. 316, which has stucco work of mythological characters by artists Abbondio Stazio and Carpoforo Mazzetti from the 1700's. Near the Rialto Bridge, the B&B San Luca is a loftlike hotel in an 18th-century palazzo. The wood-beamed rooms are edgy but classic: colorful Kartell lights, Venini vases, and Starck Ghost chairs are paired with antique wooden dressers. The hotel's only real downside is its lack of an elevator, though Paolo will be happy to carry your bags up the three flights of stairs.

If you prefer a little more luxury, there's the intimate, 12-room Ca' Maria Adele. Glamour comes naturally to the proprietors, the Campa brothers, whose grandfather created the world's largest Murano-glass chandelier (a panoramic photograph of the piece is on view in the breakfast salon). Fittingly, rooms have their own crystal chandeliers and silk wall fabrics, as well as bird's-eye views of the Santa Maria della Salute, a 17th-century church that resembles a tiered wedding cake. A favorite among privacy-craving celebs attending the Venice Film Festival, Charming House IQs has four large rooms and

Opposite, clockwise from top left: Santa Maria Mater bridge; the Skyline Bar, at the Hilton Molino Stucky hotel; designer Saviero Pastor carving wooden oarlocks in his workshop, Le Forcole; ravioli filled with shrimp, pumpkin, and ricotta at Osteria Alle Testiere.

suites that are done up with contemporary furnishings by Moroso and B&B Italia in shades of chocolate, cream, and red. The hotel is only accessible by boat, and guests can expect to be lulled to sleep by the opera-singing gondoliers on the nearby canal.

Whether you want an over-the-top meal with a view of the lagoon, seafood tagliatelle at a low-key trattoria, or Venetian *cicheti* (tapas), Venice has a restaurant to suit. The 22 seats at the retro bistro Osteria Alle Testiere are among Venice's most difficult to book. Sommelier Luca Di Vita presides over the tiny *salotto*, outfitted with an antique marble-topped bar, where he advises patrons on how to pair Veneto whites. *Piatti del giorno* might include sautéed John Dory with lemon and orange and Di Vita's homemade ginger-and-vanilla gelato. Only those in the know will find their way to Antiche Carampane, concealed within a maze of winding alleys in the San Polo district. The portions have become less generous over the years, but such antipasti as sour eggplant and creamed codfish remain among the best in town. In Cannaregio, a 15-minute walk from San Marco, is Boccadoro, where as much attention is paid to the décor as to the food: the sleek dining room has steel-blue walls and photos of Venetian landscapes by local photographer Roberta Ricci.

Chef Luciano Orlandi's regional dishes include handmade basil tagliatelle with grilled tuna, tomatoes, and capers.

Perhaps no restaurant is better known—or loved—than the barrel-vaulted Da Fiore. Chef Mara Martin's deceptively simple fare is worth the splurge, from plates of deep-fried calamari, scampi, and zucchini to a dessert of pineapple soup with mint and fresh berries. The tables to book are those on the outdoor balcony overlooking the canal. On the other side of the lagoon, at the Michelin-starred Met Restaurant at the Hotel Metropole, chef Corrado Fasolato uses regional ingredients for his innovative dishes such as a delicious pear-and-sheep-ricotta mousse with raspberry gelée and red-wine sorbet.

For a more affordable option, seek out the canal-side Il Refolo, run by Damiano Martin, son of the owners of Da Fiore. The restaurant, with its 25 candlelit outdoor tables, is the perfect setting for sampling Martin's savory pizzas; try the *prosciutto crudo*, mozzarella, and green-fig pie, available seasonally. But if you're planning a picnic by the lagoon, stock up on provisions at ProntoPesce. The delicatessen specializes in seafood to go: spiced couscous with mussels and mixed vegetables, oyster platters, and smoked-swordfish croissants.

After dinner, everyone looks to indulge a little. For a sweet bite, head to Alaska, a hole-in-the-wall parlor where owner Carlo Pistacchi serves up his unusual flavors of gelato—artichoke, fig, and ginger. Lines too long? Dried fruits, truffles, and 100 varieties of chocolate fill the shelves at Drogheria Mascari, the top grocery store in town.

Visiting Venice without going to Harry's Bar is almost sacrilege. The crowds may be overwhelming, but people-watching doesn't get better than at this 1931 venue, a favorite with A-listers during the film festival. Later, young locals go to the no-frills bars around the Rialto Market. Among the most popular is Naranzaria, with a bottle-stacked bar illuminated by Ingo Maurer lights and outdoor chairs that overlook the Grand Canal. For a panoramic view of the city, head to the Skyline Bar, in the Hilton Molino Stucky hotel. Here, youthful professionals and artsy types sip glasses of Campari soda and Prosecco before slipping into Ca' d'Oro alla Vedova, Venice's most authentic osteria, for lightly spiced meatballs.

Day or night, the city's labyrinthine network of islands, bridges, pedestrian alleys, and canals can be dizzying to even the most seasoned visitor. And therein lies its beauty: afternoons spent wandering the piazzas and encountering the amalgamation of influences—Roman, Byzantine, Ottoman, and Italian—at every turn. If you need a Modernist reprieve from all that history, the Museo della Fondazione Querini Stampalia is worth a stop. In the 1960's, the Veneto-based architect Carlo Scarpa refurbished part of the 16th-century palace, incorporating walls of washed concrete and travertine and a tranquil Japanese-inspired garden; the building now houses a collection of paintings by Pietro Longhi. But many of Venice's age-old treasures lie out of doors. To teach travelers about the ecological challenges facing the city, the sustainable-tourism venture Context Travel organizes guided walking tours that highlight Venice's preservation efforts.

The hidden islands that surround the city offer their own kind of education. The most efficient way to explore them is by private charter. *Il Nuovo Trionfo*, a double-masted 1926 sailing vessel, is available for small groups. Don't miss the island of San Michele and its Renaissance-era church, where you can pay your respects at the tombs of Stravinsky and other luminaries, such as Ezra Pound. You'll also want to spend a day visiting the island of Murano, full of tiny boutiques selling the area's signature glassware; Marina e Susanna Sent is a local favorite.

Which is to say there's more to shopping in Venice than kitschy plastic gondolas. Looking for a rare edition of John Ruskin's *Stones of Venice*? Old World Books carries English-language volumes about Venice bought at auctions and private sales. The city is also brimming with an eclectic mix of handmade accessories and clothing, along with fabric, leather, and wooden goods from area craftsmen. Senegal-born Moulaye Niang's store Muranero sells contemporary jewelry that uses the bright colors of his homeland, such as bulbous glass rings in orange and lilac. You'll find legendary designer Mariano Fortuny's fabrics at the Fortuny Factory & Showroom, where 16,000 yards of Egyptian cotton are handcrafted every year. And the 62-year-old workshop Legatoria Polliero is the place for notebooks, wrapping paper, photo frames, and unique handmade papers made using a collection of 300 antique Asian printing blocks.

Architect Francesca Meratti is on a mission to bring Venetian design into the 21st century. Her contemporary boutique, Madera, stocks steel and ceramic casseroles by Italian designer Rodolfo Dordoni for KnIndustrie; minimalist aprons by Inzu that double as halter-necked pinafore dresses; and finely sculpted wooden bowls from Meratti's own line. And while an oarlock might not be at the top of your shopping list, once you step inside the woodworking shop Le Forcole you're likely to change your mind. Designer Saviero Pastor hand-carves sinuous, one-of-a-kind pieces in walnut, cherry, or pear wood. In fact, the works are so stunning, they've been snapped up as sculptures by I. M. Pei.

Milan may be Italy's fashion capital, but Venice has a style all its own. The clothing shop Hibiscus carries boho-chic pieces such as kimono jackets and flared knee-length silk skirts in rouge and rust. Since 1968, milliner Giuliana Longo has been creating signature hats in her workshop. Pick up a brightly colored beret made of rabbit fur and felt. During periods of *acqua alta* (high water), opt for a pair of high-heeled rain boots in splashy red at Dittura Massimo. When the waters retreat, slip your feet into a custom pair of shoes by avant-garde shoemaker Giovanna Zanella. Her wild designs run the gamut from lace-up boots in green and pink leather to frog-skin flats perfect for exploring the city's cobblestoned streets on foot. After all, Venice's present-day charms are easy to come by—if you know where to look. ✚

Opposite, from left: *Preziosi di bassa marea,* a dish of assorted seafood, at Hotel Metropole's Met Restaurant; chef Corrado Fasolato.

resources

STAY

B&B San Luca Campo della Chiesa, San Marco 4066; 39-041/241-2614; sanluca-bb.com; doubles from $.

Bauer Il Palazzo San Marco 1459; 800/223-6800 or 39-041/520-7022; bauerhotels.com; doubles from $$$$.

Ca' Maria Adele Rio Terà dei Catecumeni, Dorsoduro 111, 39-041/520-3078; camaria adele.it; doubles from $$.

Ca' Sagredo Campo Santa Sofia, Cannaregio 4198-99; 800/525-4800 or 39-041/241-3111; casagredohotel.com; doubles from $$$.

Charming House IQs Campiello Querini Stampalia, Castello 4425; 39-041/ 241-0062; thecharming house.com; doubles from $$$.

Cipriani Giudecca 10; 800/237-1236 or 39-041/520-7744; hotelcipriani.com; doubles from $$$$$.

Hotel Danieli Castello 4196; 800/325-3589 or 39-041/522-6480; luxurycollection.com; doubles from $$$.

Hotel Gritti Palace Campo Santa Maria del Giglio; 800/325-3589 or 39-041/794-611; luxurycollection.com; doubles from $$$.

Oltre il Giardino Fondamenta Contarini, San Polo 2542; 39-041/275-0015; oltreilgiardino-venezia.com; doubles from $$.

EAT

Alaska Calle Larga dei Bari, Santa Croce 1159; 39-041/715-211; ice cream for two ✗.

Antiche Carampane Rio Tera delle Carampane, San Polo 1911; 39-041/524-0165; dinner for two ✗✗✗.

Boccadoro Campiello Widmann, Cannaregio 5405A; 39-041/521-1021; dinner for two ✗✗✗.

Da Fiore Calle del Scaleter, San Polo 2202A; 39-041/721-308; dinner for two ✗✗✗✗.

Drogheria Mascari Calle degli Spezieri, San Polo 381; 39-041/522-9762; snacks for two ✗.

Il Refolo Campo San Giacomo de l'Orio, Santa Croce 1459; 39-041/524-0016; dinner for two ✗✗.

Met Restaurant Riva degli Schiavoni, Castello 4149; 39-041/524-0034; dinner for two ✗✗✗✗.

Osteria Alle Testiere Calle del Mondo Novo, Castello 5801; 39-041/522-7220; dinner for two ✗✗✗.

ProntoPesce Pescheria Rialto, San Polo 319; 39-041/822-0298; dinner for two ✗✗.

DRINK

Ca' d'Oro alla Vedova Ramo Ca' d'Oro, Cannaregio 3912; 39-041/528-5324; drinks for two ✗.

Harry's Bar Calle Vallaresso, San Marco 1323; 39-041/528-5777; drinks for two ✗.

Naranzaria Erbaria, San Polo 130; 39-041/724-1035; drinks for two ✗.

Skyline Bar Giudecca 810; 39-041/272-3310; drinks for two ✗.

DO

Context Travel 39-06/976-25204; contexttravel.com.

Il Nuovo Trionfo Cannaregio 6025; 39-041/522-7075; ilnuovotrionfo.it; boat rentals from $$$$ for up to 30 people.

Museo della Fondazione Querini Stampalia Campo Santa Maria Formosa, Castello 5252; 39-041/523-4411.

SHOP

Dittura Massimo Calle Nueva Sant'Agnese, Dorsoduro 871; 39-041/523-1163.

Fortuny Factory & Showroom Giudecca 805; 39-041/528-7697.

Giovanna Zanella Campo San Lio, Castello 5641; 39-041/523-5500.

Giuliana Longo Calle del Lovo, San Marco 4813; 39-041/522-6454.

Hibiscus Ruga Rialto, San Polo 1060/1; 39-041/523-7486.

Le Forcole Fondamenta Soranzo, Dorsoduro 341; 39-041/522-5699.

Legatoria Polliero Campo dei Frari, San Polo 2995; 39-041/528-5130.

Madera Campo San Barnaba, Dorsoduro 2762; 39-041/522-4181.

Marina e Susanna Sent 20 Fondamenta Serenella; 39-041/527-4665.

Muranero Salizada del Pignater, Castello 3545; 39-338/450-3099.

Old World Books Ponte del Ghetto Vecchio, Cannaregio 1190; 39-347/512-9695.

ATENEO VENETO

On Campo
San Fantin.
Opposite:
Minimalist
wares at
the Madera
studio.

TIPS FROM THE TASTEMAKERS

For many visitors to Europe, the ultimate luxury is authenticity. And there's no better place to find it than in the wisdom of a local, someone willing to share his or her passion or particular expertise. Here, three creative trailblazers reveal their insider secrets—the places that usually go unmentioned in the guidebooks.

Lisbon Music Tour

WHAT Fado, a melancholic style of acoustic music dating back to the 1820's, is still an intrinsic part of the Portuguese culture, with performance spots sprinkled around the capital.

WHO Mariza is the iconoclastic diva of the country's traditional fado scene. "I've performed at so many venues that it's hard to choose a favorite," she says.

SEE After dark, **Clube de Fado** *(94 Rua São João da Praça; 351/21-885-2704; clube-de-fado. com)*, an intimate restaurant in Alfama, Lisbon's oldest neighborhood, becomes a local haunt for up-and-coming *fadistas.* **A Tasca do Chico** *(39 Rua Diario de Noticias; 351/96-505-9670)*, a small beer hall in Bairro Alto, hosts Fado Vadio (street fado) nights twice a week, where amateurs are encouraged to take the stage. Don't let the seemingly shady surroundings of **Fábrica Braço de Prata** *(1 Rua da Fábrica do Material de Guerra; 351/96-551-8068; bracodeprata.net)*, in the docklands, deter you from an evening visit. The 1908 arms factory is home to a cultural center consisting of exhibition spaces, a cinema, a bar and café, a bookstore, and a courtyard hosting concerts. The Saturday-at-midnight fado is a must.

EAT Try the just-caught grilled fish, vegetarian soufflés, and thick-cut steaks at **XL** *(57 Calçada da Estrela; 351/21-397-2486; dinner for two XXX)*, in Baixa/Chiado.

DRINK The outdoor terrace makes **Xafarix** *(69 Avda. Dom Carlos I; 351/21-395-1395)* an ideal spot to sip a glass of port while listening to live music.

Helsinki Design Watch

WHAT Chairs, vases, rugs, wallpaper—the Finns have always done it with style.

WHO "With its Modernist designs and small islands just off the coast, Helsinki tends to inspire creative minds," says Ville Kokkonen, design director of Artek, the Finnish furniture company cofounded by Alvar Aalto in 1935.

SEE From Market Square, take a ferry to **Suomenlinna** *(suomenlinna.fi)*, an 18th-century island fortress and UNESCO World Heritage site. Explore the huge granite ramparts before heading to the cliffs for an unforgettable Baltic vista. The national **Design Museum** *(23 Korkeavuorenkatu; 358-9/622-0540; design museum.fi)* exhibits the best homegrown and international talent in fashion, industrial, and graphic design. **Aalto House** *(20 Riihitie; 358-9/481-350; alvaraalto.fi)* is a shrine to the Modernist era. A minimalist white box, it contains many of Aalto's iconic, sculptural pieces.

EAT Start with the *puuro* (porridge) at **Café Ekberg** *(9 Bulevardi; 358-9/6811-8660; breakfast for two XX)*. For Finnish specialties such as pike cake with pickled-cucumber sauce, visit **Juuri** *(27 Korkeavuorenkatu; 358-9/635-732; lunch for two XX)*, in Kantakaupunki. **Ateljé Finne** *(14 Arkadiankatu; 358-9/493-110; dinner for two XXX)*, a former sculptor's studio in the Töölö area, serves local dishes such as elk sausage and stuffed Baltic herring.

SHOP When it comes to vintage shopping, the Kruununhaka district is unbeatable. **Vanhaa Ja Kaunista** *(6 Liisankatu; 358-9/135-2993)* sells tumblers by Aino Aalto (Alvar's first wife).

Florence Art Walk

WHAT The birthplace of the Italian Renaissance has become a hot spot for contemporary creativity.

WHO J.K. Place Hotels founder Ori Kafri, a photography collector and gallerist. "Artists are trying to comprehend the present while relating to the past," he says. "Florence provides an ideal context."

SEE Kafri's by-appointment photography and video showroom, **FOR Gallery** *(33R Via dei Fossi; 39-055/215-457; forgallery.it)*, is in Diladdarno, the city's emerging art district. It's dedicated to cutting-edge talent such as Israeli street-art photographer David Kassman and Italy's Massimo Listri. Nearby, the long-established **Poggiali e Forconi** *(35A Via della Scala; 39-055/287-748; poggialieforconi.it)* has hosted rotating shows, including those by Patti Smith and David LaChapelle. **Museo Marino Marini** *(Piazza San Pancrazio; 39-055/219-432; museomarino marini.it)*, in a former church, houses 183 sculptures and paintings by Marini, a mid-20th-century Tuscan artist famous for stylized equestrian works. Art guru Isabella Brancolini oversees

Clockwise from left: A streetcar on Rua da Conceição, in Lisbon's Baixa district; Massimo Listri's 2007 photo of Castello di Govone, showing at FOR Gallery, in Florence; Ville Kokkonen, design director of Artek; Alvar Aalto's 1937 tea trolley; Brancolini Grimaldi bookstore and gallery, in Florence; gallerist Ori Kafri. Opposite: Portuguese fado performer Mariza.

the *centro storico*'s **Brancolini Grimaldi** *(12R Vicolo dell'Oro; 39-055/239-6263; brancolini grimaldi.com)*, a bookstore and gallery that shows international photography. In the basement of a Renaissance palazzo, the **Strozzina** cultural center *(Piazza Strozzi; 39-055/277-6461; strozzina.org)* showcases themed exhibits by young area artists.

SLEEP Architect Michele Bönan designed Kafri's stylish, 20-room **J.K. Place Firenze** *(7 Piazza S.M. Novella; 39-055/264-5181; jkplace.com; doubles from $$$)* with thoughtful residential touches—large bookcases; welcoming fireplaces.

DRINK Creative types flock to the pocket-size **Art Bar** *(4R Via del Moro; 39-055/287-661; drinks for two $)* for its fresh-fruit cocktails.

PRAGUE'S BOHEMIAN REVIVAL

BY MARIA SHOLLENBARGER
PHOTOGRAPHED BY MONIKA HOEFLER

The city and the Vltava river, as seen from Prague Castle.

T HE CAPPUCCINO I'M DRINKING IN PRAGUE'S GRAND Café Orient is utterly mediocre, and that's okay.

That is because the point is really the setting, which is by contrast utterly impressive: the café is on the second floor of the House of the Black Madonna, originally constructed in 1912 as a department store by the Czech Cubist architect Josef Gočár and, as of 2003, home to Prague's Museum of Czech Cubism, an architectural and design movement that emerged, flourished, and faded away here in the course of about 15 years. After being neglected for decades, the Orient was restored in 2005 to its original, rigorously angled splendor. Everything is a faithful replica of what once was: polished-brass and silk-shaded lamps are suspended from the white-beamed ceiling; glossy, geometric woodwork surrounds the mirrored bar; half-octagon banquettes are covered in a flawless reproduction of the original green-and-white upholstery. Once visited by scholars and architecture aficionados, today the café is a map-marked stop on many a hipster's list and the tables around me are occupied by good-looking young locals and a smattering of travelers. Barring their presence, the room is a veritable time capsule of a place that existed here, and only here, for little over a decade almost a century ago.

Which is why the subpar coffee's not such a problem—considering that the promise of a good cup lies all around me at any number of Italian cafés or Starbucks-like chains in the city's Old Town. But the loving restoration of the Grand Café Orient and, equally important, the warm reception it has received from Prague's own citizens speak to something interesting: a renewed affection among Czechs for their own heritage and traditions, whether of Bohemia or of the 20th century.

And it is a new sensibility, a change from the city's years-long, full-throttle embrace of foreign cultures and far-flung influences—a preoccupation that was perhaps to be expected in a country whose borders were thrown open so abruptly in 1989. As travelers' expectations—fed by the burgeoning 1990's phenomena of increasingly affordable airfare and the proliferation of *Wallpaper* culture for growing numbers of self-styled jet-setters—grew to include the inalienable right to have, say, pitch-perfect northern Italian cuisine or an "it" bag (or a faultless cappuccino) no matter where on the planet they were touching down, so Prague developed by leaps and bounds to meet those expectations. Local entrepreneurs and canny foreigners alike were keen to invest in this new European capital that was evolving so promisingly. By 2001, the city offered cappuccinos in spades, a few "it" bags, and, for good measure, a Four Seasons Hotel set on the Vltava River with the Michelin-starred Allegro restaurant (still the best in the city, serving that impeccable northern Italian, natch).

After watching their city achieve the trappings of global-destination status, however, a handful of creative residents have begun mining Prague's own traditions—of food, art, design, architecture—for inspiration. And they've been subtly but tangibly changing the look and feel of the city ever since.

One of the earliest to see the promise of Prague's indigenous culture was Janek Jaros, who for almost a decade has been championing Czech Cubism from his downtown gallery Modernista. Set somewhat incongruously among the treacly gift boutiques and garnet sellers along Celetná, a popular tourist road in Old Town, Modernista is Prague's original Czech design emporium. The

fortysomething Jaros manufactures reproductions of furniture, kitchenware, and porcelain by the best-known Czech Cubists, such as Vlatislav Hofman, Pavel Janák, and Josef Gočár (of the House of the Black Madonna), and sources hard-to-find originals for a handful of prominent clients, among them London's Victoria & Albert Museum. But it's only in the past three years that his local clientele—relatively newly educated about their own aesthetic traditions, and ready to invest—has begun to grow. "Modernista has changed a lot in the last three years, and so has the market. We're going back to basics, working with locals and expatriates who live in Prague long term."

Jaros also collaborated with the designers of the Rocco Forte Collection's 101-room Augustine hotel by helping to source products for its interiors. Housed in a 13th-century Augustinian monastery spread over seven buildings in the picturesque Malá Strana district, the hotel offered Olga Polizzi, the collection's design director, a chance to delve into Prague's visual history. "What's unique about the Czech Cubists is that they pushed the ideas of Picasso and Braque beyond what the movement in Western Europe was producing," she says. "In Prague, Cubism became buildings, decorative objects, printing, textiles. It's a very important—perhaps *the* most important—period in Czech art."

Known for her work on Rome's polished Hotel de Russie and the renovation of Rocco Forte's London flagship, Brown's, Polizzi committed herself to integrating local design traditions into the Augustine's interiors. The results are a testament to how an international hotel brand can achieve an authentic sense of place in one property. Few European hotels can match the Augustine, with its still-active ecclesiastical libraries and 18th-century frescoes, for pedigree (the Mandarin Oriental, Prague, just blocks away and also housed in a former monastery, is one). Some of the textiles in the rooms are faithful reproductions of archival Cubist and Modernist designs; others are more playful interpretations of them. Hofman's signature armchairs and dining chairs were purchased in bulk from Jaros, so that most rooms have one (along with a selection of tomes and catalogues on Czech Cubist theory and objects). Porcelain pieces—vases, boxes, tea saucers—line bookshelves. A sinuous reclined chaise longue by another significant Czech Modernist, the Brno-born architect Adolf Loos—whose well-preserved

Villa Müller in Prague's green Střešovice suburb is open to visitors—appears in some of the suites. All of this interacts dynamically with rough stone, pitched chestnut beams, somber portraits of saints, and biblical scenes from the order's private collections that Polizzi had restored and hung in the stairwells. The effect: two vernaculars sharing Czech DNA but separated by 6½ centuries. "The rigor of Cubism, of its aesthetic, lends itself well to this strict environment," Polizzi says. "And they're both quintessential parts of the city."

Across the river on the edge of Old Town, just down the street from Jaros's Modernista, an American expat named Karen Feldman is busy reinterpreting one of the city's other great artistic traditions: hand-etched glassware and crystal. Feldman left San Francisco for Prague in the early 1990's and soon developed a keen interest in top-quality glass workmanship. In 1999, she founded Artěl, which produces contemporary glassware hand-engraved by classically trained artisans (many descended from generations in the same trade). She started the business in the bedroom of her apartment; a decade later, her products—characterized by bold or abstracted takes on traditional motifs, and the occasional tongue-in-cheek one (swirling goldfish, underwater scenes, jellyfish, and sea horses included)— are sold at Barneys in Tokyo and at Paul Smith in London and New York City. In the Artěl boutique, on Celetná, rows of symmetrical spotlighted alcoves are filled with highballs and flutes. Glass cases lining the walls hold tableware and jewelry, including gem-toned sunburst rings and pendants. There's a deftly edited selection of vintage objects along with contemporary pieces produced by young Czech design entrepreneurs, such as Maxim Velčovský, of the firm Qubus, a definitive presence on the Prague creative scene, and Olgoj Chorchor, a collective whose work is sold at Moss, in New York City.

"There's definitely new interest among many Czechs in their aesthetic history," Feldman says. She talks of Velčovský, a provocateur and dandy, whose Qubus atelier, a warmly lit and cheery space behind massive iron-studded wooden doors, is a few blocks away. He similarly plays with traditional craft techniques made thought-provoking with healthy doses of irony. (Feldman quotes him as telling her he's "selling up parts of his childhood" with his design output, which includes porcelain sculptures—a pair of rain boots; a bust of

Lenin; a bowl in the shape of the old Czechoslovakia—embossed with the traditional Bohemian *zwiebelmuster*, or blue onion, pattern.)

She also cites Prague's premier fashion designer, Klára Nademlýnská, who plays up her Paris training over any professions of Bohemian inspiration, but in whose structured, uncomplicated designs one occasionally sees a flourish of peasant-style embroidery or a shape (a shepherd's hood, for example) that speaks to a memory of some regional sartorial history. (Certainly the total disinclination to serve that prevails among the lissome, unsmiling girls in her shop on Dlouhá Street is a holdover from the old country.)

Feldman takes me one night for a dining experience she says is a 21st-century Czech phenomenon that draws from the past. La Degustation Bohême Bourgeoise (or Degustation, as it is known) was a revelation for Czechs as well as visitors to the city when it opened in Old Town in 2006. Executive chef and co-owner Oldřich Sahajdák assembled a nine-person team comprising some of Prague's top internationally trained talent, variously poached from the city's best restaurants (sous-chef Marek Šáda came from Kampa Park; *chef du pâtissier* Lukáš Pohl was formerly at Café Savoy) and lured home from abroad (sommelier Kristýna Janičková has worked at Gordon Ramsay at Claridge's and Alain Ducasse at the Dorchester in London). Their mandate: Revive and add a contemporary twist to the haute cuisine traditions of late-19th-century well-to-do Bohemia.

The seven-course meal is filled with dumplings—pheasant dumplings are served with wild poultry soup and quail egg, and barley dumplings come alongside poached beef oyster blade. It's also gratifyingly couth, with traditional sauces recast as essences (and, yes, foams) and spectacular, almost architectural presentation. Equally refined are the room itself, with its low, barrel-vaulted ceilings, and the open kitchen, tiled in black and white and squadroned by an enfilade of grinning young sous-chefs who look to be having the time of their lives.

When queried on Prague's changing visual arts scene, Feldman and Jaros—who are, as it happens, two of the city's most articulate ad hoc ambassadors—both urge a visit to Dox, the buzzy contemporary-arts center that opened in 2008. One of the first exhibits in this sprawling 1920's metal factory (redesigned by the contemporary Czech architect Ivan Kroupá) was the enormous installation called *Entropa*, by Czech artist David Černý. A 40-foot-high mosaic suspended on a pipe system, with steam whistles and moving parts, it's a wild map of the 27 EU member states: Romania is a Dracula-themed park; the Netherlands a flooded plain dotted with half-submerged mosques; Italy one enormous soccer pitch on which players run chaotically. It was commissioned to be exhibited at the European Council building in Brussels for the duration of the Czech presidency, but generated so much controversy that it was dismantled and sent back to Prague—to the dismay and amusement of art-savvy Czechs, who could have told any well-meaning Eurocrat that Černý, a self-styled *enfant terrible*, was not the guy for such a serious-minded job. (In the aftermath of the Velvet Revolution, he painted a Soviet tank cotton-candy pink and affixed a huge raised middle finger atop it.) Post-controversy, Černý admitted that the 27 artists he'd listed as collaborators—one from each EU country—were all fictitious; the work was his and that of two associates.

Entropa is provocative, and definitely Czech, and Dox couldn't have gotten luckier to land such a piece within months of opening, notes Leoš Válka, the gallery's director. In a city of slightly twee costume, crystal, and folk museums, the sprawling, multilevel Dox is a pioneer, not only because Válka chose to set it in Holešovice, a grimy grid of blocks to the north of the city that's populated by students, immigrants, and

Above:
Designer Klára
Nademlýnská
in her shop on
Dlouhá Street.

Opposite: Dox,
a former metal
factory turned
contemporary
art gallery.

aspiring artists keen on its cheap rents. "The idea behind Dox is to place Czech artists in a world context, across the contemporary disciplines—visual art, architecture, new media, design," Válka says. It's a new format for the city, and one that potential supporters are still acclimating to. "We haven't got the history of privately funded activities, of philanthropy, and the government's still coming up to speed with how to manage its grants," he explains. Nevertheless, he adds, "our timing's been extremely good; people here have been traveling, they've gone and cultivated perspectives on [contemporary] art elsewhere in the world." They're ready, in other words, to appreciate their own contemporary artists.

Feldman has also recommended a tour of the four-year-old Lobkowicz Palace Museum, which enjoys a rather more rarefied position high above the city in the Prague Castle complex. It was opened in 2007 by William Lobkowicz, a Boston native who also happens to be a prince by title of what was for five centuries Bohemia's most powerful and wealthiest family. Its fortunes having been dispersed and its landholdings seized not once but twice, first by the Nazis, then the Communists (his grandfather, Maximilian, fled Czechoslovakia in 1948), they are now being meticulously traced, gathered, and catalogued by Lobkowicz and his wife, who have lived in Prague for 20 years.

The museum is stunning, a world-class collection lent intimacy by its placement in the family's residence (a late-Renaissance palace, overlooking castle vineyards and the rooftops of Malá Strana) and by an audio tour written and presented by Lobkowicz himself. Masterpieces such as Peter Brueghel the Elder's *Haymaking* and two galleries hung entirely with ancestral portraits by the likes of Velázquez are the marquee attractions. But equally captivating are the smaller dramas, such as hand-scrawled sheaves of music from Beethoven's Third Symphony, a jewel-like ladies' salon with 200-year-old murals of exotic birds, and case after velvet-lined case of family porcelain, much of it painted in the same blue-onion pattern that Qubus's Velčovský has twisted ever so slightly to his own creative purposes.

Lobkowicz's love for his adopted city is palpable, his investment in it total, and his perspective on it unique—that of both an outsider and a member of its most established society. This is likely why his view of things is a long one: It's great that there's a renewed enthusiasm for the country's own culture manifesting itself, he explains, but he wasn't particularly worried about it disappearing. "Prague has always been a mosaic; it's maintained an open-minded energy for a thousand years," he says. "The city is never going to lose itself." ✚

resources

STAY

The Augustine 12/33 Letenská; 888/667-9477 or 420/266-112-233; theaugustine.com; doubles from $$.

Four Seasons Hotel Prague 1098/2A Veleslavínova; 800/332-3442 or 420/221-427-777; fourseasons.com; doubles from $$$.

Mandarin Oriental 459/1 Nebovidská; 866/526-6567 or 420/233-088-888; mandarinoriental.com; doubles from $$$.

EAT

Allegro 2A/1098 Veleslavínova; 420/221-427-000; prix fixe dinner for two ✖✖✖✖✖.

Angel 7 Kolkovně; 420/773-222-422; dinner for two ✖✖✖.

Céleste Tancici Dun, 80 Rašínovo Nábřeží; 420/221-984-160; dinner for two ✖✖✖.

Degustation 18 Haštalská; 420/222-311-234; prix fixe dinner for two ✖✖✖✖✖.

Grand Café Orient 19 Ovocný; 420/224-224-240; coffee and cake for two ✖.

DO

Artěl Glass 29 Celetná; 420/224-815-085; artelglass.com.

Dox 34 Osadní; 420/774-145-434; doxprague.org.

House of the Black Madonna (Museum of Czech Cubism) 19 Ovocný; 420/224-211-746; ngprague.cz.

Klára Nademlýnská 3 Dlouhá; 420/224-818-769.

Lobkowicz Palace Museum 3 Jiřká, Prague Castle; 420/602-595-998; lobkowiczpalace.cz.

Modernista 12 Celetná; 420/224-241-300; modernista.cz.

Prague Castle Castle District; 420/224-372-422; hrad.cz.

Qubus 3 Rámová; 420/222-313-151; qubus.cz.

Villa Müller 14 Hradním Vodojemem, Strešoviče; 420/224-312-012; mullerovavila.cz.

DESIGN PILGRIMAGES

These days, cutting-edge architecture is everywhere you look—and it's not limited to major cities.
From innovative bridges to industrial-chic wineries, thoughtful, inventive design can lure travelers to places they
never expected to visit. Here, seven contemporary icons that are becoming destinations in themselves.

Covilhã, Portugal

High-style pedestrian bridges are popping up all over: Central Europe's longest was unveiled in Szolnok, Hungary, in 2011, and residents of Copenhagen are looking forward to the 2012 completion of the Cirkelbroen. But the most impressive of all may be here, 186 miles northeast of Lisbon, where minimalist architect João Luis Carrilho da Graça's streamlined walkway zigzags high above the Carpinteira river valley. At night, the warm wood paneling that lines its interior is illuminated from below, imbuing the bridge with a romantic glow.

Oxford, England

The monumental transformation of the 17th-century **Ashmolean Museum**, the oldest public museum in the United Kingdom, is exceedingly discreet: the new building, designed by Rick Mather Architects, maintains a low profile behind the Ashmolean's beloved 19th-century Greek Revival façade. It is through here that visitors still enter, before flowing into a skylighted atrium. The museum's collections now enjoy twice the display space, and two undulating staircases ensure that natural light filters vertically via interconnecting, double-height galleries. 44-1865/278-000; ashmolean.org.

Liège-Guillemins, Belgium

More than any other working architect, Santiago Calatrava has made the sheer drama of geometry and engineering his trademark, and his high-speed-train **EuroGare** station, in Liège-Guillemins, is no exception. Spanning 518 feet under a sloping, bubble-like canopy made of steel, glass, and white concrete, the structure gleams from within and appears to have emerged from the surrounding urban fabric like an emblem of the future that was always meant to be there. sncb.be.

Gudbrandsjuvet, Norway

A series of glass-and-wood boxes scattered across a mountainside in the north-western part of the country, the **Juvet Landscape Hotel** looks to be the result of some sort of high-modern architectural airdrop maneuver. Designed by Jensen & Skodvin Architects, each stand-alone guest room has floor-to-ceiling windows overlooking beautiful, rugged terrain and nothing else. The effect: total immersion in nature. 47/9503-2010; juvet.com; doubles from $$.

Weil am Rhein, Germany

Furniture manufacturer Vitra's grassy headquarters, at the meeting point of France, Germany, and Switzerland, has been an architecture destination since its Frank Gehry–designed museum opened in 1989. There are also buildings by Zaha Hadid and Tadao Ando, but the most remarkable sight may be the **VitraHaus** showroom designed by Herzog & de Meuron. The Swiss firm has taken the archetypal pitched-roof house, elongated it, and stacked 12 of them up like fireplace logs. Inside, you can follow winding staircases through the dreamlike space as you browse for home furnishings. vitra.com.

Burgenland, Austria

The "Wine Architecture" movement has placed stunningly modern wineries in all of Austria's grape-growing regions. However, Burgenland, about an hour southwest of Vienna, has the lion's share. Examples include the angular **Esterhazy**, near Eisenstadt, by Anton Mayerhofer; the sleek **Leo Hillinger**, in Jois, by Gerner Gerner Plus; and the **Arachon Winery**, in Horitschon, with its dramatically angled stone archway, by Wilhelm Holzbauer and Dieter Irresberger. For a full list, consult the Austrian Wine Marketing Board at austrianwine.com.

Lodz, Poland

A sister property of the ultramodern Andel's Hotel in Prague, the Polish version is notable for its setting, an immense red-brick mill built by the 19th-century Jewish entrepreneur Izrael Poznanski. The **Andel's Hotel Lodz** is just one component of a fantastic cultural and shopping district that somehow escaped destruction during World War II. An electrical plant from 1912 is now a dance club; an ornate 1877 weaving mill houses restaurants and stores. And, in a former finishing mill, you'll find the **Museum of the Factory**. 48-42/279-1000; andelslodz.com; doubles from $$.

Clockwise from above: Three pitched-roof showrooms at VitraHaus, in Germany; Andel's Hotel Lodz's Maisonette Deluxe room; Santiago Calatrava's EuroGare railway station, in Belgium; the pedestrian bridge in Covilhã, Portugal; a room overlooking the Valldøla River at Norway's Juvet Landscape Hotel; the Ashmolean Museum, in England. Center: The entrance to Austria's Arachon Winery.

ST. PETERSBURG MODERN

BY VALERIE STIVERS-ISAKOVA
PHOTOGRAPHED BY FRANK HERFORT

Capturing a shot of the Golden
Peacock clock in St. Petersburg,
Russia's Hermitage Museum.
Opposite: Lounging at Terrassa
Restaurant, next to Kazan Cathedral.

A PRODUCT OF THE IMAGINATION—AND IRON will—of Peter the Great, St. Petersburg has always taken creative cues from the glories of Western Europe, its Neoclassical colonnades standing in stark contrast to its onion-domed churches. In fact, the forward-thinking czar envisioned his imperial capital in 1703 as a window into Europe, and it has long been a center of culture and sophistication, with some of the world's best art and ballet. The Soviet years were hard on St. Petersburg, and its ties with the Continent were cause for official suspicion—and neglect. But now the edgy, intellectual little sister to big-money Moscow is in the midst of a style revival that's breathing new life into hotels, restaurants, and shops, creating a flashy backdrop for nouveau riche residents and visitors alike.

Photographer turned hotelier Oksana Kurenbina took inspiration from the work of local artists for the 25 rooms at Antique Hotel Rachmaninov, a hub for creative types that occupies two floors of a Soviet-era apartment building just off Nevsky Prospekt, St. Petersburg's main promenade. Across the Moyka Canal, the W St. Petersburg, the brand's first foray into Eastern Europe, features 137 modern rooms with floor-to-ceiling windows, and lamps in the shape of gilded disco balls, all set in a 19th-century building. This corner near the Hermitage is also home to the five-room Casa Leto B&B, which has a residential style. Guests share a small living room and a dining area and are attended to by the friendliest staff in town (most unusual in Russia). But if a fresh take on czarist glamour seems like a better fit, request one of the 17 new Terrace rooms at the 1875 landmark Grand Hotel Europe, overlooking Mikhaylovsky Palace. At its Art Nouveau lobby bar—once frequented by Dostoyevsky—order your vodka neat, the way the locals do. And just across the Neva River on Vasilỳevsky Island, an up-and-coming arts neighborhood, the Finnish owners behind Sokos Hotel Palace Bridge are banking on their nautical rooms to lure travelers off the beaten path.

The St. Petersburg dining scene has moved well beyond caviar and blini. The words *espresso* and *double latte* are everywhere, and in the city center, sushi and sashimi saturation is complete. A decade after chef-entrepreneur Aram Mnatsakanov opened his groundbreaking modern Italian restaurant Probka, the Russian cognoscenti still maintain an insatiable appetite for haute-global cuisine. In-the-know Petersburgers craving Indian head to sultry Botanika for vegetarian samosas and ginger-spiked dal, and interiors courtesy of local designer—and cult DJ—Alexey Haas. Meanwhile, prolific restaurant group Ginza Project has launched three notable hot spots. Terrassa, a glass-walled space next to Kazan Cathedral, serves a mix of Italian, Thai, and Russian dishes (chicken-liver risotto, *tom yum* soup, and marinated herring share top billing on the eclectic menu). At the Asian-fusion Luzhayka, or "lawn" in Russian, the theme is whimsical wonderland: the restaurant's pet rabbits roam the grounds, and children can fish in a pond surrounded by open-air dining cabanas. Across town, riverboat restaurant *Volga-Volga* trolls the Neva serving up views of the golden spires of the Peter and Paul Fortress while waiters bring on the mâche salad with seared tuna and sturgeon soup.

Restaurants aren't the only markers of change. In the new Moscow-styled St. Petersburg, young people are looking less and less like refugees from a Slayer concert. The boutique that most embodies

Opposite, clockwise from top left: The LowFat Studio showroom; a sign of the times at a central bus stop; performing bike tricks in front of the Hermitage; rooftop dining at Loft Project Etagi's Green Room.

the city's hip new zeitgeist is LowFat Studio, an open-door workshop and showroom for the eco-friendly fashion line developed by business partners Merya and Vera Dmitriyeva. The innovative duo, who design playful items such as unisex loungewear, stock a refrigerator with seasonal snacks for shoppers (gooseberries in spring; ice cream bars on hot summer days). Another stop for souvenirs beyond the ubiquitous matryoshka dolls is Lyyk Design Market, a white-on-white space in a hidden courtyard that features Russian fashion designers' avant-garde looks. Across town, Generator Nastroenia—the name translates to "mood generator"—lifts spirits with leather journals embossed with tongue-in-cheek Russian-language jokes or Soviet-propaganda-themed covers, a token of the city's past.

The city's leading arts venue, Loft Project Etagi, is accessed by a hidden stairwell that leads to three galleries, a bookstore, and four spaces for major international exhibitions. Further delighting modern art lovers are two museums, both on Vasilyevsky Island, that opened in 2010. Erarta, set in a 20th-century columned building on the western edge of the island, focuses on up-and-coming Russian talent. Novy Museum, near the island's metro stop, displays paintings and sculptures from genre-defining artists including Sots-Art duo Komar & Melamid.

For a similar feel back on the mainland, there are eclectic galleries Rosphoto and 100 Svoih, set above a basement bar that's known for sets by underground DJ's. If it's emerging talent from the world of classical music you're interested in, head to the Concert Hall at the Mariinsky Theatre, where the winners of the city's Tchaikovsky competition, which takes place every four years, perform during the White Nights festival, a celebration of music and ballet, held from May through July.

During the summer, there's plenty to do outside of town, too. St. Petersburg is an ideal jumping-off point for cruising. New options include the Grand Princes of Russia itinerary with Academic Arrangements Abroad, a New York–based operator affiliated with the Metropolitan Museum of Art. Tours are geared toward serious arts aficionados, but the trip—including seven days on the redesigned *Volga Dream* riverboat—is open to all. A more adventurous choice is a 10-day cruise to the White Sea's Solovetsky Islands led by Infoflot. The accommodations are bare-bones, but it is the best way to see the remote archipelago and its wild coastline, as well as the main island's Solovetsky monastery. Like many remnants of the Soviet era (it was formerly held by the Soviet gulag), the monastery is a fitting reminder of just how far St. Petersburg has come. ✚

resources

STAY

Antique Hotel Rachmaninov 5 Kazanskaya Ul.; 7-812/571-7618; hotelrachmaninov.com; doubles from $.

Casa Leto B&B 34 Bolshaya Morskaya Ul.; 7-812/600-1096; casaleto.com; doubles from $$.

Grand Hotel Europe 1/7 Mikhaylovskaya Ul.; 7-812/329-6888; grandhoteleurope.com; doubles from $$.

Sokos Hotel Palace Bridge 2/4 Birzhevoi Per.; 7-812/335-2200; sokoshotels.fi; doubles from $$.

W St. Petersburg 6 Voznesensky-Prospekt; 877/946-8357; whotels.com; doubles from $$.

EAT

Botanika 7 Ul. Pestelya; 7-812/272-7091; dinner for two ✕✕.

Luzhayka 16 Aptekarsky Prospekt; 7-812/324-7094; dinner for two ✕✕.

Probka 5 Ul. Belinskogo; 7-812/273-4904; dinner for two ✕✕✕.

Terrassa 3A Kazanskaya Ul.; 7-812/937-6837; dinner for two ✕✕.

Volga-Volga Petrovsky Nab., Dock 1; 7-812/900-8338; dinner for two ✕✕.

SHOP

Generator Nastroenia 7 Karavannaya Ul.; 7-812/314-5351; generator-nastroenia.ru.

LowFat Studio 17 Vilensky Per.; 7-812/579-2639; lowfatwear.com.

Lyyk Design Market 74 Nab. Kanala Griboyedova; 7-812/939-6051; lyyk.ru.

DO

Academic Arrangements Abroad 800/221-1944; arrangementsabroad.com; 14 days from $$$$$ per person.

Concert Hall at the Mariinsky Theatre 37 Ul. Dekabristov; 7-812/326-4141; mariinsky.ru.

Erarta 2, 29-ya Liniya; 7-812/324-0809; erarta.com.

Infoflot 7-495/684-9188; infoflot.ru; from $$$$$ per person.

Loft Project Etagi 74 Ligovsky Prospekt; 7-812/458-5005; loftprojetetagi.ru.

Novy Museum 29, 6-ya Liniya; 7-812/323-5090; novymuseum.ru.

100 Svoih 39 Ligovsky Prospekt; 7-812/719-9517; 100svoih.ru.

Rosphoto 35 Bolshaya Morskaya Ul.; 7-812/314-1214; rosphoto.org.

Strolling across
the San Paternian
bridge, in
Venice, Italy.

contributors

Luke Barr
Thomas Beller
Anya von Bremzen
Dominique Browning
Jennifer Chen
Swazi Clarity
Jennifer Cole
Simon Doonan
Mark Ellwood
Amy Farley
Andrew Ferren
Lucy Firestone
Mary Firestone
Erin Florio
Jennifer Flowers
Eleni N. Gage
Charles Gandee
Alice Gordon
Farhad Heydari
Catesby Holmes
Tina Isaac

Karrie Jacobs
Nathalie Jordi
Stirling Kelso
Peter Jon Lindberg
Heather MacIsaac
Charles Maclean
Alexandra Marshall
Ralph Martin
Christopher Mason
Heidi Mitchell
Shane Mitchell
John Ryan Poynter
Dorkys Ramos
Bruce Schoenfeld
Maria Shollenbarger
Gary Shteyngart
Valerie Stivers-Isakova
Valerie Waterhouse
Stephen Whitlock
Sarah Wildman
Ingrid K. Williams

A typical traffic jam on
an Icelandic country road.

photographers

Cedric Angeles
Simon Brown
Martha Camarillo
David Cicconi
Blasius Erlinger
Andrea Fazzari
Roberto Frankenberg
Jean Paul Guilloteau/Express-REA/Redux
Robert Harding Picture Library Ltd./Alamy
Frank Herfort
Monika Hoefler
Christian Kerber
John Kernick
Max Kim-Bee
Yadid Levy/Anzenberger/Redux

Rebecca Lewis
Martin Morrell
Morgan & Owens
David Noton Photography/Alamy
Pegaz/Alamy
Mischa Richter
Myriam Roehri
Jessica Sample
Zubin Shroff
Jonathan Skow
Christopher Simon Sykes
Frank Tophoven/Laif/Redux
Richard Truscott
Susan Wright

TRAVEL+LEISURE
EUROPE THE PLACES WE LOVE

Editor Jennifer Miranda
Consulting Editors Laura Begley Bloom, Irene Edwards, Peter J. Frank
Art Director Wendy Scofield
Photo Editor Beth Garrabrant
Production Associate David Richey
Editorial Assistant Dorkys Ramos
Copy Editors David Gunderson, Mike Iveson, Ed Karam, Sarah Khan, Libby Sentz
Researchers Tomás Martín, Charles Moore, Paola Singer

TRAVEL + LEISURE
Editor-in-Chief Nancy Novogrod
Creative Director Bernard Scharf
Executive Editor Jennifer Barr
Managing Editor Laura Teusink
Arts/Research Editor Mario R. Mercado
Copy Chief Kathy Roberson
Photo Editor Whitney Lawson
Production Director Rosalie Abatemarco-Samat
Production Manager Ayad Sinawi

AMERICAN EXPRESS PUBLISHING CORPORATION
President and Chief Executive Officer Ed Kelly
Chief Marketing Officer and President, Digital Media Mark V. Stanich
CFO, SVP, Corporate Development and Operations Paul B. Francis
VP, General Managers Keith Strohmeier, Frank Bland
VP, Books and Products Marshall Corey
Director, Book Programs Bruce Spanier
Senior Marketing Manager, Branded Books Eric Lucie
Assistant Marketing Manager Stacy Mallis
Director of Fulfillment and Premium Value Philip Black
Manager of Customer Experience and Product Development Charles Graver
Director of Finance Thomas Noonan
Associate Business Manager Uma Mahabir
Operations Director Anthony White